D1307873

# KOREA:

## THE
## UNKNOWN
## WAR

K O

# R E A

## THE UNKNOWN WAR

### JON
### HALLIDAY
### AND
### BRUCE
### CUMINGS

PANTHEON BOOKS
NEW YORK

First American Editon

Copyright © 1988 by Jon Halliday and Bruce Cumings.

All rights reserved under International and Pan-American Copyright
Conventions. Published in the United States by Pantheon Books, a division of
Random House, Inc., New York, and simultaneously in Canada by Random
House of Canada Limited, Toronto. Originally published in Great Britain
by Viking.

Library of Congress Cataloging-in-Publication Data

Halliday, Jon.
    Korea : the unknown war.

    Includes index.
    1. Korean War, 1950-1953.    I. Cumings, Bruce,
1943-        .  II. Title.
DS918.H23    1988        951.9'042        88-42717
ISBN 0-394-55366-7

Manufactured in the United States of America

Designed by Jessica Smith

Maps and charts by Chapman Bounford and Associates

*Frontispiece: Women at Taegu army depot watching as their menfolk go off for
training in the South Korean Army, summer 1950.*

# CONTENTS

405334          WEST GEORGIA REGIONAL LIBRARY SYSTEM

# ACKNOWLEDGEMENTS

We would like to thank Thames Television for permission to use material developed in the course of the making of the television series *Korea: The Unknown War*.

We would like to thank the following people for help in obtaining photographs: Michael Brunton, at the London office of *Life*; Konrad Ege for research in Washington, DC; Israel Epstein and Paul White for help in Beijing; Chris Marker for allowing us to use his unique photographs of North Korea, in spite of many vicissitudes; Pang Sun Joo; Lucjan Pracki; Jack Saunders; and Nina Prescod for photographs in London. Our thanks are due to the following libraries in London for allowing us to copy materials in their possession: Royal Institute of International Affairs; School of Oriental and African Studies, University of London; School of Slavonic and East European Studies, University of London.

Simon Duke did valuable archival research for the TV series, which was of great help to us.

We would particularly like to thank our agent, Anthony Sheil, the book's designer Jessica Smith, and Kate Atkinson, Tony Lacey and Tessa Strickland at Viking for acute editorial help – and patience.

J.H. wishes to acknowledge a debt of gratitude to Jung Chang for help beyond words.

J.H. and B.C.
January 1988

# CHRONOLOGY

| | |
|---|---|
| *c.* AD 700 | United Korean state |
| 1905–10 | Japanese takeover; annexation 1910 |
| 1919 | Uprising, 1 March |
| 1932–45 | Guerrilla resistance by communists |

**1945**

| | |
|---|---|
| 8 August | USSR enters war against Japan; fights in Korea |
| 15 August | US General Order No. 1 calls for USA to take Japanese surrender in Korea south of thirty-eighth parallel; USSR accepts |
| August–September | People's committees set up, leading to central government – Korean People's Republic – based on Seoul |
| 8 September | First US troops arrive |
| end September | Kim Il Sung returns to Korea |
| 16 October | Syngman Rhee returns to Korea |
| 12 December | USA bans people's committees |
| 27 December | Foreign Ministers' Conference (USA, USSR, UK), Moscow, agrees plan for Korean independence |

**1946**

| | |
|---|---|
| 20 March–8 May | US–Soviet Joint Commission meets in Seoul – deadlock (reconvenes May–October 1947) |
| October–November | Mass uprisings in South Korea |

**1947**

| | |
|---|---|
| end September | USSR proposes simultaneous withdrawal of own and US troops; USA takes Korea issue to UN |

**1948**

| | |
|---|---|
| April | Uprising on Cheju Island |
| 19–23 April | National Conference in Pyongyang, attended by most political leaders of North and South except Rhee, opposes US–UN plan for separate elections in South (held 10 May) |
| 15 August | Republic of Korea inaugurated in Seoul; Rhee proclaimed President |

| 9 September | Democratic People's Republic of Korea inaugurated in Pyongyang; Kim Il Sung proclaimed premier |
| 20 October | Mutinies and uprisings in South lead to guerrilla warfare (which continues until 1950) |
| 25 December | Red Army withdraws (advisers remain) |

**1949**

| March | Kim Il Sung visits Moscow |
| 30 June | USA withdraws troops (advisers remain) |
| August | Fighting across thirty-eighth parallel intensifies |

**1950**

| February | Sino–Soviet Agreement |
| April | NSC–68; Dulles appointed to handle East Asia |
| 30 May | Elections in South; setback for Rhee |
| 17 June | Dulles arrives in Seoul (stays until 21 June) |
| 25 June (24 USA) | Full-scale fighting begins |
| 25 June (USA) | UN Security Council meets at USA's request |
| 26 June | US Air Force and Navy intervene |
| 27 June | Truman declaration of intervention in Korea and China; UN recommends intervention |
| 28 June | Seoul falls; Zhou Enlai calls US action 'armed aggression' |
| July–August | KPA takes 90 per cent of South |
| 15 September | Inchon landing leads to reinstatement of Rhee |
| 30 September | Zhou says, 'We will not stand by . . .' |
| 1 October | South Koreans cross thirty-eighth parallel; USA follows (and reaches border with China on 26th) |
| 2 October | China decides to enter war (first troops in action on 25th; major attacks on 27 November) |
| 30 November | Truman suggests that A-bomb might be used |
| 16 December | State of Emergency declared in USA |

**1951**

| | |
|---|---|
| end January | Maximum southward point of Chinese Volunteers' and Korean People's Army's advance |
| 1 February | UN condemns China as 'aggressor' |
| 11 April | MacArthur fired; heavy fighting (until June) |
| 10 July | Peace talks open at Kaesong (and move to Panmunjom in October) |
| 8 September | Western treaty with Japan; 'Operation Hudson Harbor' (dummy A-bombs) |

**1952**

| | |
|---|---|
| February–June | POW uprisings on Koje lead to massacres |
| 25 May | Rhee introduces martial law; USA considers plan to oust Rhee ('Operation Everready') |
| 23 June | Power plant on Yalu bombed |
| October | Eisenhower: 'I shall go to Korea' (he goes 2–5 December) |

**1953**

| | |
|---|---|
| 2 February | Eisenhower's State of the Union speech 'unleashes' 7th Fleet (Mao replies on 7 February, 'We are not intimidated') |
| 5 March | Stalin dies; intensive Moscow talks |
| 13–16 May | USA bombs dams near Pyongyang; gigantic flooding |
| 19 July | USA stands as guarantor for Rhee |
| 27 July | The armistice is signed |
| 26 October | Tripartite pre-Political Conference talks at Panmunjom (USA walks out on 12 December) |

**1954**

| | |
|---|---|
| 26 April–15 June | Geneva Conference on Korea |

**1958**

Last Chinese troops leave Korea

# INTRODUCTION

The Korean war of 1950–53 was the most important war ever fought between the West and communism. It saw sixteen armies from all five continents deployed under US command and the UN flag against two armies, those of North Korea and China. It brought the people of Korea appalling destruction, devastation and tragedy; there were millions of deaths and more millions of divided families. Yet it is still an unknown war, with unravelled mysteries and continuing evasions by the major belligerents. Both sides claim to have won, yet both actually seem to feel they lost.

Korea is one of the oldest nations on earth, with a rich culture, more than a millennium of unity and an indisputable national identity. In 1945, after nearly four decades of harsh Japanese colonial rule, it was divided and denied its independence by outside powers; its people were not consulted. The USA occupied the South between 1945 and 1948, while the Russians occupied the North. Separate republics emerged on both sides of the thirty-eighth parallel in 1948, each claiming to be the legitimate Korean sovereign, yet Korea was universally recognized as a single nation, and no party in Korea, nor any international body, endorsed the national division.

The question most often asked about the Korean war is 'Who started it?' No one asks who started the Vietnam war, or the civil war in China. Yet all these conflicts were the same in essence – a civil war fought between two domestic forces: a revolutionary nationalist movement, which had its roots in tough anti-colonial struggle, and a conservative movement tied to the *status quo*, especially to an unequal land system. What was different in Korea was the form and timing of outside intervention.

Unlike the other two conflicts, that in Korea is treated by many Western commentators as though it were a black hole in outer space, where a war just happened to happen. Because it came at the height of the Cold War, and because of near-complete ignorance of the internal forces playing upon Korean society, an entire literature treats the war as a bolt out of the blue in June 1950, with unknown or irrelevant antecedents. Even today the enemy side, in particular, remains an opaque Never-never-land, undeserving of inquiry. Those who did dig beyond the surface – the American journalist I. F. Stone, for example, or some of Britain's best reporters, like James Cameron, René Cutforth and Reginald Thompson – often got into trouble as a result.

We have sought to give an idea of the kind of war it really

was. The photographs in this volume bear eloquent testimony to a reality different from that of a United Nations 'police action' against Soviet-sponsored aggression, of unshaven American soldiers freezing in God-forsaken mountains to fight 'hordes' of Chinese. Indeed, the undeniable witness of those on the scene – not just courageous investigative reporters but also photographers from mass magazines such as *Life* – was to a people's war: kids or grandmothers pulling guns from their 'white pyjamas', guerrillas fighting well before and well after June 1950, people working in caves and underground factories to sustain a peasant society against the greatest power on earth.

The people of Korea suffered worst in this war, especially civilians in the North, who had to live three years under the heaviest and most sustained bombing ever known, and the millions of refugees who wandered desperately across the blasted landscape of their beautiful country. Nearly 35,000 American soldiers died fighting in Korea, a fearful toll. But more than 3 *million* Koreans died, a horrendous slaughter that touched every family. This story too is obscured in conventional accounts, but not in photographs from the time.

There was bravery and courage in this war, as always. There was also cruelty, callousness and racism. There was censorship and deceit. We have tried to give a succinct all-round picture of what happened, bridging the gap between the conflicting and incomplete evidence on both sides.

The pictures we have selected represent images that formed people's consciousness in the West and images that were not seen at that time – if they had been, they might have made people think more deeply, or even differently, about the war. In particular, the illustrations show how the war was represented by different participants and observers: Korean, American, British, Chinese and Russian.

The text draws upon recently declassified archival documentation and interviews with an unprecedentedly broad range of participants – ranging from Dean Rusk to the late Emanuel Shinwell and the CIA's key Korea specialist at the time the war started, Korean and Chinese soldiers, seven people who met Kim Il Sung in his underground bunker in Pyongyang and top figures in the Soviet and American administrations of Korea in 1945–8. We have written a longer work on the same subject, *The Fire in Korea*,* where our claims are fully documented and referenced. We hope that readers who are interested in pursuing the subject further will consult our other volumes.

*Published by The Bodley Head in Britain and Pantheon in the USA. Readers can also consult Bruce Cumings's two-volume study, from which his contribution to both books is drawn: *The Origins of the Korean War* (Princeton University Press, vol. I, 1981; vol. II, forthcoming).

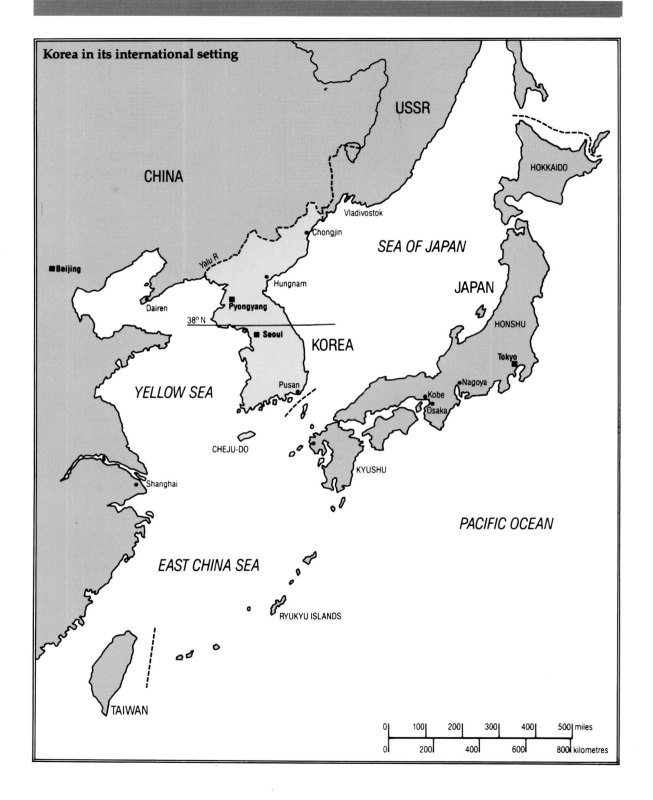

Korea in its international setting

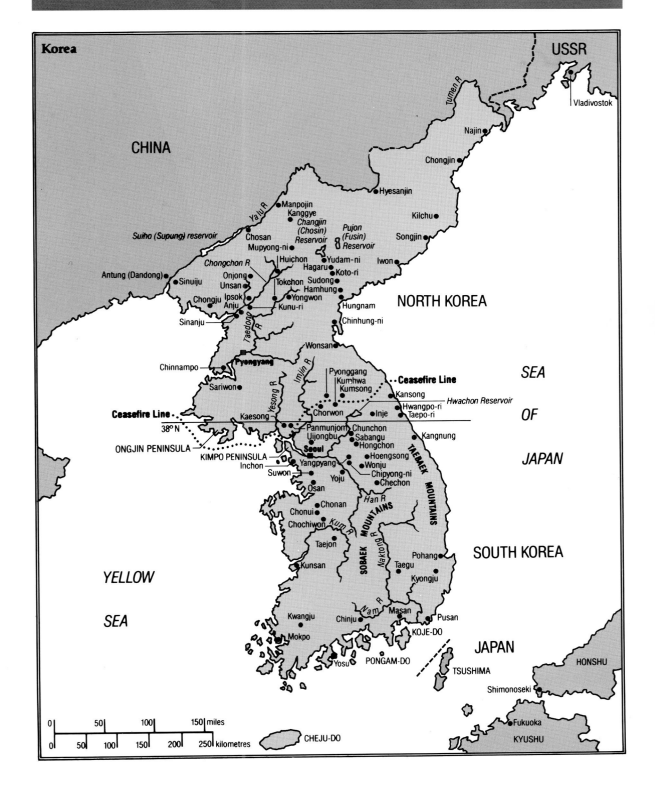

Korea

USSR

CHINA

NORTH KOREA

SOUTH KOREA

JAPAN

SEA

OF

JAPAN

YELLOW

SEA

Vladivostok

Najin

Chongjin

Hyesanjin

Kilchu

Tumen R.

Manpojin
Kanggye
Changjin
(Chosin)
Reservoir
Pujon
(Fusin)
Reservoir
Songjin

Yalu R.

Suiho (Supung) reservoir
Chosan
Mupyong-ni
Huichon
Hagaru
Yudam-ni
Koto-ri
Iwon

Chongchon R.
Onjong
Unsan
Tokchon
Sudong
Hamhung
Antung (Dandong)
Sinuiju
Chongju
Ipsok
Anju
Kunu-ri
Yongwon
Sinanju
Hungnam
Chinhung-ni

Taedong R.

Wonsan

Chinnampo
Pyongyang
Sariwon

Yesong R.

Imjin R.

Pyonggang
Kumhwa
Kumsong
Kansong
Ceasefire Line
Hwachon Reservoir
Chorwon
Inje
Hwangpo-ri
Taepo-ri

Ceasefire Line
38° N
Kaesong
Panmunjom
Uijongbu
Chunchon
Sabangu
Hongchon
Kangnung
ONGJIN PENINSULA
KIMPO PENINSULA
Inchon
Yangpyang
Suwon
Seoul
Hoengsong
Wonju
Chipyong-ni
Chechon
Yoju
Osan

Han R.

Chonui
Chochiwon
Chonan

Kum R.

SOBAEK MOUNTAINS

TAEBAEK MOUNTAINS

Naktong R.

Taejon
Kunsan
Pohang
Taegu
Kyongju

Nam R.

Kwangju
Chinju
Masan
Pusan
Mokpo
KOJE-DO
JAPAN
HONSHU
Yosu
PONGAM-DO
TSUSHIMA
Shimonoseki

Fukuoka
KYUSHU

0     50     100     150 | miles
0   50  100  150  200 | 250 | kilometres
CHEJU-DO

13

# OUTSIDE INTERVENTION AND A DIVIDED KOREA

Korea entered the twentieth century as an agrarian bureaucratic kingdom of half a millennium's duration. Although deeply influenced by China and nominally its dependency, it had been a unified, independent nation stretching back more than a thousand years. Its foreign policy, one of strict seclusion, had led to the country's being known as the 'Hermit Kingdom'. For a quarter of a century after 1876, however, the peninsula had been the object of rivalry among several imperial powers: Russia, Japan, the United States and Britain. Japan ended this rivalry by defeating Russia in 1905, proceeding to make Korea its colony in 1910. The United States and the Soviet Union ended the period of colonial rule by defeating Japan in 1945. Thus Korea has been shaped historically by its indigenous traditions and, in recent decades, by the influence of Japan, the USA and the USSR; China has been a traditional and influential omnipresence.

The remarkable persistence of Korea's political culture springs from its unique homogeneity, resulting from a coincidence of nation, race and ethnicity and its long-term isolationism. The equally remarkable changes of this century derive ultimately from Korea's involvement with the modern world system that began – and has not yet completed – the transformation of the old Hermit Kingdom. Although North Korea is the revolutionary state on the peninsula, its foreign and domestic policies have many traditional roots; although South Korea is the conservative state, its wide-ranging economic involvement with the rest of the world daily transfigures the ancient continuities.

The USA and the USSR presided over Korea's national division in 1945, but Japan has probably been the greater influence in this century. It held Korea for nearly half a century, pursuing a Janus-style colonialism that both destroyed and created: obliterating Korea's national independence and its self-governing state while building a modern bureaucracy, discriminating against Koreans racially while giving them modern education as good imperial subjects, rewarding collaborators while punishing all but the most moderate forms of resistance, exploiting the economy to Japan's benefit while building an advanced structure of roads, railroads, ports and new industries. This intense experience has gnawed at the Korean national identity ever since and spawned the forces that have swayed post-war Korea: nationalist and communist resistance movements, with many of their leaders exiled from Korea; a modern economic, military

The caption to this *New York Times* photograph, dated 20 March 1950, noted that this guerrilla in the South was 21 years old and had been captured with thirty-seven partisans. All the women in the group were 'later photographed each holding the severed head of their former chiefs'.

**Japanese police with hooded Korean prisoners, *c.* 1910 (Japan annexed Korea in 1910).**

**Trial of participants in the 1 March 1919 uprising, the biggest protest against Japanese rule over Korea. Between 1 million and 2 million people took part, and some 7,000 Koreans were killed.**

**Women students demonstrating, Seoul, 1919.**

and bureaucratic elite, unfortunately tainted by collaboration; a mass of peasants and workers who were deeply dislocated by the Pacific war; and the forced-pace industrialization of the last decade of colonial rule.

Just before Koreans heard the voice of Emperor Hirohito, for the first time, broadcasting Japan's surrender and Korea's liberation on 15 August 1945, John J. McCloy of the American War Department directed two young colonels, Dean Rusk and Charles H. Bonesteel, to withdraw to an adjoining room and find a place to divide Korea. Given thirty minutes to do so, they chose the thirty-eighth parallel because, as Dean Rusk told us, it would 'place the capital city in the American zone'. The Russians, who had begun to fight the Japanese in Korea on 8 August, accepted the division in silence. American forces arrived from Okinawa in early September, and Korea began the most anomalous period in its history since AD 668 – the era of national division, not yet ended.

Many Americans express surprise when they learn that US involvement with Korea came well before 1950, in a three-year occupation (1945–8) in which Americans operated a full military government. A. M. Rosenthal, former editor and now a regular columnist of *The New York Times*, wrote in 1986 that 'the government of Korea' functioned throughout the peninsula in 1945 but was undermined by Americans who stupidly let the Russians come into the North. This is exactly backwards. An ostensible Korean government did exist within a few weeks of Japan's demise; its headquarters was in Seoul, and it was anchored in widespread 'people's committees' in the countryside. But this Korean People's Republic (formed on 6 September 1945) was shunned by the Americans. It was the Soviets who 'let' the Americans come into the South and who supported the people's committee network. The American preference was for a group of

16

Kim Ku, President of the Korean Provisional Government in exile, *seated, c.* 1932; standing is Yun Pong-gil, who threw a bomb that killed and maimed several top Japanese officials in Shanghai in 1932. Kim Ku took over the leadership of the exiled Provisional Government from Syngman Rhee, who was expelled in 1925 for embezzlement. The Provisional Government stayed in (Nationalist) China until 1945, when its leaders returned to Seoul.

General John R. Hodge
and Cardinal Francis
Spellman aboard the
command ship *Catoctin* –
the ship that took
Roosevelt to Yalta – as it
negotiated Inchon harbour
on 8 September 1945.

**Elements of the US 7th
Infantry Division march
to the Capitol from
Seoul's railway station,
8 September 1945.**

**Kim Il Sung,** *third from
left, rear,* **with a group of
anti-Japanese guerrillas,** *c.*
**1937. Kim started fighting
the Japanese in north-east
China in about 1932. The
communist guerrillas in
China were the main
Korean anti-Japanese
resistance force, and Kim
and his guerrilla
colleagues formed the core
of the leadership in
northern Korea after 1945.**

conservative politicians who formed the Korean Democratic Party (KDP) in September 1945, and so the occupation spent much of its first year dismantling the committees in the South, which culminated in a major rebellion in October 1946 that spread over several provinces.

In October 1945 both military commands sponsored welcoming ceremonies for two returned exiles: Syngman Rhee, who later became the first President of the Republic of Korea (ROK), and Kim Il Sung, subsequently premier of the Democratic People's Republic of Korea (DPRK). Within a few months they were the dominant figures in the two zones. Rhee was a septuagenarian who had lived in the USA for nearly four decades, had a Ph.D. from Princeton and had taken an Austrian wife; a patriot well known for devoting his life to Korean independence, he was also a wilful

19

The first Korean to die in the political violence of liberated Korea. Shot by Japanese police as Americans landed on 8 September, he was either labour union leader Kwon Pyong-gun or peace-keeping activist Yi Sok-ku, both of whom were killed that day.

man of legendary obstinacy and strong anti-communist beliefs. Kim Il Sung had begun armed resistance in the Sino–Korean border region shortly after Japan established the puppet state of Manchukuo in 1932 and was fortunate enough to survive a rugged guerrilla war that had killed most of his comrades by 1945. Kim was 33 years old when he returned, and represented a younger generation of revolutionary nationalists filled with contempt for the failure of their fathers and determined to forge a Korea that could resist foreign domination. Although both leaders had the support of a superpower, neither was an easily malleable puppet.

The ROK was not proclaimed until 15 August 1948; none the less the Southern political system was built in the first few months of the occupation and did not change substantially until the 1960s. Under American auspices Koreans captured the colonial government and used its extensive and penetrative apparatus to preserve the power and privilege of a traditional land-owning elite, long the ruling class of Korea but now tainted by its associations with the Japanese. The one reliable and effective agency of this restoration and reaction was the Korean National Police (KNP). The effective opposition to this system was very broad and almost wholly on the left; a mass popular resistance from 1945 to 1950 mingled raw peasant protest with organized union activity and, finally, armed guerrilla resistance in the period 1948–50.

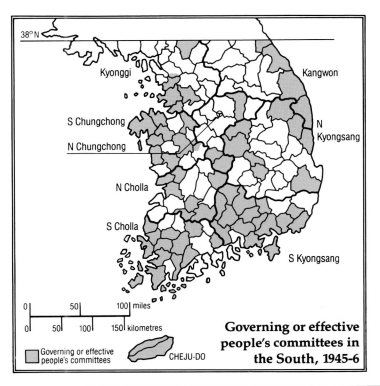

38° N

Kyonggi

Kangwon

S Chungchong

N Chungchong

N Kyongsang

N Cholla

S Cholla

S Kyongsang

0  50  100 miles

0 50 100 150 kilometres

Governing or effective people's committees

CHEJU-DO

**Governing or effective people's committees in the South, 1945-6**

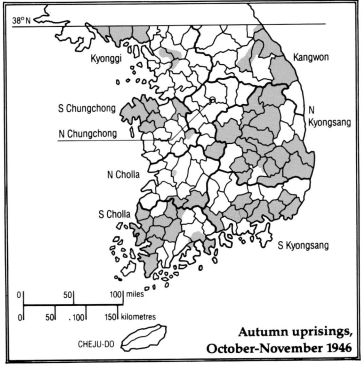

38° N

Kyonggi

Kangwon

S Chungchong

N Chungchong

N Kyongsang

N Cholla

S Cholla

S Kyongsang

0  50  100 miles

0 50 .100 150 kilometres

CHEJU-DO

**Autumn uprisings, October-November 1946**

21

US and Soviet troops meet in Korea at the town of Songdo, probably in September 1945.

US and Soviet delegates at the first session of the Joint Commission, Seoul, 30 March 1946. Standing in front are General John R. Hodge, Commander US forces in Korea, and Colonel-General Terentyi Shtykov, head of the Soviet delegation; in the centre, behind Shtykov, is Major-General Nikolai Lebedev.

A demonstration in the South, 31 December 1945. The demonstrators are protesting against trusteeship, which had just been agreed at the tripartite (UK, USA, USSR) Moscow Conference of Foreign Ministers. The Conference called for the setting up of a national government, but the Soviet–American trusteeship was widely regarded as signifying that there would not be immediate independence for Korea.

Central Intelligence Agency (CIA) analyses in 1948 bear out this picture. South Korean political life was, it said, 'dominated by a rivalry between rightists and the remnants of the left-wing people's committees', which it termed a 'grassroots independence movement which found expression in the establishment of the people's committees throughout Korea in August 1945', led by 'communists' who based their right to rule on the resistance to the Japanese. The leadership of the right, on the other hand,

> is provided by that numerically small class which virtually monopolizes the native wealth and education of the country . . . Since this class could not have acquired and maintained its favored position under Japanese rule without a certain minimum of 'collaboration', it has experienced difficulty in finding acceptable candidates for political office and has been forced to support imported expatriate politicians such as Syngman Rhee and Kim Ku. These, while they have no pro-Japanese taint, are essentially demagogues bent on autocratic rule.

The South did have a police state, and it was an agent of a small class of landlords. But it was more than that, or it could not have survived even to June 1950. The landlord class contained both obtuse reactionaries and vibrant capitalists. Korean capitalism had formidable practitioners, of which Kim Song-su, scion of a wealthy landed family, founder of Korea University, early textile industrialist, leader of the conservatives, was the most

23

formidable. His opportunities had depended on close association with the colonial regime, but his aristocratic dignity had militated against unseemly pro-Japanism. Kim Song-su and people like him laid the foundations for the economic growth of the 1960s and thereafter.

Syngman Rhee and Kim Song-su were traditional leaders concerned with organizing the elite. Those political leaders in the South who succeeded in organizing masses of people drew upon the same sources of strength as did those in the North: an appeal to complete unity at home and resistance to penetration from abroad, an assertion of a Korean essence against all the rest. These leaders included self-described rightists such as Yi Pom-sok, leader of the powerful Korean National Youth, and An Ho-sang, Rhee's first Minister of Education. Thus in 1947 a mass politics of the right emerged, resting on myriad youth groups, an incipient corporatist organization of the working class and a set of Korean political ideas that were a kind of home-grown fascism.

Of all the existing groups on the right, the North-west Youth was the most virulent. US intelligence pronounced it 'a terrorist group in support of extreme right-wing political figures'; at the beginning 'the members had all been refugees from North Korea, with real or imaginary grievances against the Soviets and the Korean communists'.

It was this brand of terror that led to the assassination of Yo Un-hyong in July 1947, by then called 'the most shot-at man in South Korea'. He had reflected the aspirations of the great majority of the Korean people in 1945 and in his person embodied the peculiar class structure of Korean society as it emerged from the Japanese grip: at home with the vast peasantry, he also had a bit of the bourgeois gentleman about him. He was an ardent nationalist and the most vocal critic of the retention of hated Korean police who had done Japanese bidding. As the CIA later acknowledged, he was the only non-communist Southern leader capable of challenging Syngman Rhee for power. Yo Un-hyong remains about the only politician from the 1940s who is honoured in both South and North Korea.

American policy, of course, never set out to create one of the worst police states in Asia. In late 1947 General John R. Hodge, commander of the occupation, captured in his homespun way the essence of the American dilemma, as it fluctuated between the unhappy poles of supporting Rhee because he was anti-communist and opposing native leftists, while hoping for a liberal outcome for which Korean society had no base:

> We always have the danger of fascism taking over when you try to fight communism. It is a very difficult political situation that we run into. Germany was built up by Hitler to fight communism, and it went to Nazism. Spain the same thing. On the other hand, when the communists build up – when communism builds up – democracy is crushed, and the nation goes communist. Now, what is the answer on the thing? How in the dickens are you going to get political-in-the-middle-of-the-road out of the mess . . . I don't know the answer. I wish I did.

**Kim Song-su, *right*, with Russell Brines of the Associated Press in February 1947. Kim was one of Korea's wealthiest men, from a family with major investments in textiles, publishing and education. He was the leading figure in the Korean Democratic Party and an important adviser to the military government. Yun Chi-yong, another important conservative leader, stands behind.**

24

Prime Minister Yi Pom-sok gives a speech, while Syngman Rhee absent-mindedly scratches his head. Yi, a key figure among pro-Nationalist Chinese politicians, was leader of the officially sanctioned Korean National Youth (September 1948).

During World War II Franklin Roosevelt had proposed a multilateral trusteeship for Korea (and for Indochina), arguing that Koreans were not ready for self-government and would have to be tutored towards an independence that would come only 'in due course'. The British and the French resisted Roosevelt's trusteeship idea, as did the Korean people, who were deeply humiliated by the prospect of yet more great-power 'tutelage'. The State Department worried about the implications of Soviet involvement in Korea for Pacific security as early as 1942 and questioned whether a trusteeship would give the USA enough influence in Korean affairs; it began to draw up plans for a full military occupation.

The USA did get the USSR to support a modified version of the trusteeship idea at the tripartite Moscow Foreign Ministers' Conference

Members of the North-west Youth welcome MacArthur to Seoul, August 1948. This was the most virulent of South Korea's youth groups, its members drawn mostly from families who had fled the North; it was responsible for systematic terrorism against the left.

Kim Kyu-sik, *left*, and Yo Un-hyong, *right*, welcome Philip Jaisohn (So Chae-pil) upon his arrival at Inchon, 6 July 1947. Hodge, fed up with Rhee's antics, thought that the ageing Jaisohn, who had been a modernizer in Korea at the turn of the century, might be a replacement for Rhee. His health failed rapidly, however, and he soon returned to the USA. Yo Un-hyong, a populist who initially led the Korean People's Republic in 1945, was felled by an assassin's bullet three weeks after this picture was taken.

in December 1945, an important agreement that suggested that the two powers might ultimately come to terms on how to reunify Korea. It shortened the period of great-power involvement in readying Korea for independence and called for a provisional government to be set up. But even by that early date the agreement came too late, because the *de facto* policies of the two occupations had identified the Soviets with Kim Il Sung and the people's committees, while the Americans backed Rhee and opposed the left and the widespread Korean demands for a thorough over-haul of the legacy of colonialism.

The Korean problem was what we would now call a 'North–South' or 'Third World' problem, a conflict over how best to overcome the debilities of colonial rule and comparative backwardness. In the Cold War milieu of the time, however, it was always seen by Americans as an East–West problem. The Soviets, we might say, pushed the North–South angle as a way of besting the USA in the East–West conflict on the peninsula. That is, they stayed in the background and let Koreans run the government; they put anti-Japanese resistance leaders out in front; and they supported radical reform of the land system, labour conditions and women's rights – all of which were pushed through by late 1946. By this time northern Korea also held its first elections for people's committees, a controlled affair that offered few choices to the electorate. The Soviets and their Korean allies acted ruthlessly against opponents of these changes, killing some, jailing others, but letting the majority of recalcitrants flee to the South. At the end

Kim Il Sung, then 33 years old, speaking at a mass rally, Pyongyang, 14 October 1945. Behind him stand General Ivan Chistiakov, commander of Soviet forces in Korea, Major-General Romanenko and Major-General Nikolai Lebedev.

Soviet officers at the 14 October 1945 ceremony, with Cho Man-sik to the right of Major-General Lebedev.

Posters in the North urging Korean self-reliance and independence, the prevention of pro-Japanese traitors from joining people's committees and support for the Moscow Agreement, November 1946.

of 1948 the Soviets withdrew their troops, leaving behind a cadre of military and government advisers and a Korean government under Kim Il Sung, who is still in control today.

The Americans could not withdraw their troops so easily because they were worried about the viability of the southern regime, its dictatorial tendencies and its frequent bluster about marching north. Korea had also become more important to American global policy as part of the new policy of containment. Acting Secretary of State Dean Acheson remarked in secret Congressional testimony in early 1947 that the USA had drawn the line in Korea and sought funding for a major programme to turn back communism there, on the model of 'Truman Doctrine' aid to Greece and Turkey. Congress and the Pentagon balked at a major commitment to Korea, however, and so Acheson and his advisers took the problem to the United Nations, hoping to contain Korea through collective security.

The United Nations was completely dominated by the USA at the time and agreed to form a committee (the United Nations Temporary Commission on Korea, or UNTCOK) to observe elections in Korea; its members included representatives of the Philippines and Nationalist China, which could be counted on to follow American direction, and representatives from Australia and Canada who, although more recalcitrant once they got a taste of South Korean politics, came from allied governments subject to American influence and pressure. The North Koreans and Soviets opposed the move to the UN and refused to participate in UN activities in Korea.

The UNTCOK-observed elections presaged a separate

Syngman Rhee at the welcoming ceremony for Allied Forces held in Seoul, 20 October 1945. Rhee had arrived back in Korea on 16 October, courtesy of Colonel Preston Goodfellow, former Deputy Director of the Office of Strategic Services. General Hodge is sitting to Rhee's right.

southern government and thus raised the issue of Korea's permanent division. For that reason virtually all the major politicians and political parties in the South refused to participate – including Kim Ku, a man probably to the right of Rhee. The election went forward none the less on a restricted franchise and boycotted by the majority of parties. The outcome, even according to several members of UNTCOK, was a foregone conclusion. The National Police and associated right-wing auxiliaries organized the voting. On 10 May 1948 the South's first National Assembly was elected, composed mostly of supporters of Rhee or Kim Song-su. After fragmentary observation of 2 per cent of the polling stations, UNTCOK endorsed the poll.

After the ROK was inaugurated, on 15 August, the State Department successfully delayed the final withdrawal of American combat troops until 30 June 1949. It then replaced them with a 500-man Korean Military Advisory Group (KMAG), established an aid mission (known as the Economic Cooperation Administration, or ECA) and pushed big aid Bills through Congress to get the Korean economy moving and to equip an army capable of defending South Korea. Meanwhile events world-wide, and especially the communist revolution in China, pushed the USA towards a formal policy of resisting further communist advances in Asia.

The ROK Army was not born at this time, however, but grew out of the Constabulary (Koreans called them National Defence Forces) that Hodge had set up in December 1945, against the orders of the Joint Chiefs of Staff. Constabulary 'detachments' were renamed 'brigades' in 1948 and then 'divisions' in 1949, but American sources reported that there were few changes in actual organization. There were six divisions at the start, led exclusively by officers who had served the Japanese – the most flamboyant of whom was Kim Sok-won.

A unit of the Korean ▷ National Police at muster, some time in 1946.

A leftist demonstrator ▷ against the separate elections being led away by police in Seoul, 1 March 1948, as rightist auxiliaries, in white, watch the crowd.

Kim Sok-won had tracked Kim Il Sung in the Manchurian wilderness in the late 1930s as the head of the 'Special Kim Detachment' in the Japanese Army. He was known then as Kaneyama Shakugen; Emperor Hirohito had decorated him with the Order of Merit for 'bravery' in campaigns in the war against China. On 2 June 1948 Kim Sok-won led 2,500 Korean veterans of the Japanese Army through the streets of Seoul, their wartime uniforms now shabby but their goose-stepping smartness still impressive. In the summer of 1949 he was Commander on the thirty-eighth parallel.

Americans knew that they had a volatile charge in Syngman Rhee, and his relations with the Embassy were often tempestuous. The most important American influence on Rhee was really his 'kitchen cabinet' of long-time associates who were almost all either Americans or Koreans who had spent years in the USA. The CIA thought that if any group succeeded in influencing this solitary President, it was the kitchen cabinet. Robert Oliver wrote many of Rhee's speeches, as did another long-time Rhee associate, Harold Noble; Oliver had far easier access to Rhee's office than did most of his cabinet ministers or, indeed, the American Embassy. Noble, from a missionary family in Korea, had worked in Army intelligence; he frequently served as a go-between in Rhee's negotiations with US Ambassador John Muccio.

**A leftist meeting at Seoul's South Mountain, 1 May 1947.**

Cho Pyong-ok talks with the Indian representative to UNTCOK, Bahadur Singh, in April 1948. The American-educated Cho was Director of the Korean National Police and an important figure in the Korean Democratic Party.

Kim Ku, *centre*, crossing the thirty-eighth parallel for the April 1948 unity conference in Pyongyang.

33

The most important American in Rhee's entourage, however, was M. Preston Goodfellow, who had been Deputy Director of the Office of Strategic Services (forerunner of the CIA) under William 'Wild Bill' Donovan and had a background in Army intelligence; like Donovan, he was known for his interest and expertise in clandestine warfare. He arranged to deposit Rhee back in Korea in 1945, sought to set up a separate Southern government in 1946 and organized guerrilla forays into the North in 1949.

Rhee was not dependent simply on the Embassy and the State Department, in other words. He reached outside the official network of relations to his paid American advisers, or to General MacArthur, or to Chiang Kai-shek, or to Republican Congressmen, or to allies in American intelligence, or to highly experienced former Japanese colonialists; this was no one-way street. Yet at the same time Rhee often seemed like a tethered hound, constantly pulling at the leash until he nearly strangled. The relationship was thus a bizarre one: the American giants sought to throw a net on this Korean Lilliputian, still worried that he would get free. Hand-wringing overlords watched a palsied gambler, none knowing for sure what was happening today, what might happen tomorrow.

The critical background to the Korean War was in the realm not of personality, however, but of the social and political conflict between left and right throughout the peninsula. This conflict went on at the national level in 1945, and at the provincial and county levels in 1946, as local people's committees fought with their antagonists. The suppression of the massive autumn harvest uprisings in 1946 consolidated state control in the county seats, making the seizure of power by county people's committees unlikely thereafter. Yet villages continued to be isolated from central power, and leftists therefore migrated downwards through the bureaucratic reaches of the system in search of space for organization.

By 1947 most leftists were members of the South Korean Labour Party (SKLP). The party was always indigenous to the South, drawing its members especially from the south-west and south-east, but it was more independent of Northern or Soviet influence in 1947 than after the formation of the Rhee government. Only vague and unreliable evidence existed on Northern or Soviet provision of funding for the party, and American intelligence sources did not believe that the North directed SKLP activity – they thought instead that the two worked towards common goals.

It appears, however, that by mid-1948, if not earlier, the party was under Northern guidance. Intercepted instructions from the North urged members to infiltrate into 'all important bureaux' of the Rhee government, secrete food and other supplies for guerrillas in the mountains and 'infiltrate into the South Korean Constabulary and begin political attacks aimed at causing dissension and disorder'. Up to the Korean war, however, it cannot be said that Southern communists were mere creatures of Kim Il Sung, and there was much conflict between the Northern and Southern parties.

Rhee and his allies formed counter-organizations at the village

Major-General William F. Dean, US Military Governor, thanks a provincial police chief for a successful rice collection, March 1948. Dean was the highest-ranking US officer captured by the North Koreans during the war.

level to fight the left. Roy Roberts of the Associated Press wrote in August 1947 that US intelligence received each day an average of five police reports 'telling of fights in villages, fights between villages, beatings of rightists, beatings of leftists, burning of granaries, attacks on village officials, attacks on police, stoning of political meetings'.

An account of one of these battles, dated 19 August 1947, from a small town near Masan, along the south-east coast, is representative. Some 1,000 peasants gathered to hear officials talk about the military government's rice-collection programme and then

> became hostile and started stoning the speechmakers. The police present were forced to fire into the mob, to give the township officials a chance to retreat across the rice fields. The retreating policemen passed a police box, and stopped long enough to secure additional rifles and ammunition. The mob overran the police box, seized documents and demolished the box completely. They then split into two parts, one part erecting road blocks, and the other destroying telephone communications.

These village battles occurred in regions of previous people's committee strength. An American intelligence survey in September 1947 found that 'an underground people's committee government exists in certain parts of South Korea'. A survey team sent to South Cholla Province termed it 'perhaps the most leftist area in South Korea'; it estimated that 15 to 20 per cent of the communities visited 'were openly hostile to the Americans. Leftist activity all over was evident . . .'

### Insurgency on Cheju

Before 1950 no place suffered the political conflicts of liberated Korea like Cheju, a beautiful volcanic island off the southern coast, where guerrilla war began in 1948. The effective political leadership on Cheju until early 1948 was provided by strong, rooted people's committees that first emerged in August 1945; General Hodge once said that Cheju was 'a truly communal area that is peacefully controlled by the people's committee without much Comintern [i.e., Soviet] influence'.

After a demonstration on 1 March 1948 against the separate elections on the mainland, the police arrested 2,500 young people, and islanders soon fished the dead body of one of them out of a river: he had been tortured to death. But the affair that most inflamed the island population was the unleashing of the North-west Youth. In late 1947 the American Counter-intelligence Corps had 'warned' this group about its 'widespread campaign of terrorism' on Cheju. But under the American command these same youths joined the police and Constabulary in guerrilla-suppression campaigns on the island. As a subsequent Korean press investigation put it:

> Since the coming of a youth organization, whose members are young men from north-west Korea, the feeling between the [island] inhabitants and those from the mainland has been growing tense . . . They may have been inspired by the communists. Yet, how shall we understand how over 30,000 men have roused themselves to action in defiance of gun and sword? Without cause, there can be no action.

The North-west Youth was said to have 'exercised police power more than the police itself and their cruel behaviour has invited the deep resentment of the inhabitants'.

The guerrillas generally were known as the *Inmin-gun*, or People's Army, estimated to be 3,000 to 4,000 strong. But they were not centrally commanded and operated in mobile units of eighty or a hundred people who often had little connection with other rebels. The Japanese had left a honeycomb of caves, tunnels and defensive bunkers on the island; in some of the caves caches of small arms had also been left, which the guerrillas used. They hid in these emplacements, striking from mountains that commanded the coastal road and low-lying villages. By early June 1948 most villages in the interior were controlled by the guerrillas; roads and bridges were destroyed throughout the island.

By the end of 1948 the ROK authorities had recorded 102 battles, more than 5,000 combatants on both sides, nearly 6,000 islanders in custody and a claimed total of 422 dead insurgents. By April 1949 20,000 homes on the island had been destroyed, and one-third of the population (about 100,000) was concentrated in protected villages along the coast. By the end of April the American Embassy reported, 'The all-out guerrilla extermination campaign . . . came to a virtual end in April with order

**Guerrillas captured on Cheju Island, May 1948.**

restored and most rebels and sympathizers killed, captured, or converted.' Some American sources thought that between 15,000 and 20,000 islanders died in the conflict, but the ROK news agency reported a figure of 33,000; the North Korean figure was 30,000. This amounted to about 12 per cent of the island population.

Children being relocated on Cheju Island, May 1948. Most, if not all, villages in the interior were evacuated to coastal areas, to separate the people from the guerrillas.

Displaced people on
Cheju.

### The Yosu Rebellion

As the Cheju insurgency progressed, an event occurred that received much more attention: a rebellion at the port city of Yosu that soon spread to other counties in the south-west and south-east and that, for a time, seemed to threaten the foundations of the fledgling republic. The cause of the uprising was the refusal, on 19 October 1948, of elements of the 14th and 6th Regiments of the republic's Army to embark for a mission against the Cheju guerrillas. By dawn on 20 October the rebels (numbered then at 2,000) had seized control of Yosu; some elements then entrained for Sunchon and took it over by the early afternoon, overwhelming police reinforcements. Soon rebels had spread out to near-by towns.

Within hours of the regimental revolt, large numbers of people were parading through Yosu, waving red flags and shouting slogans; at a mass meeting on 20 October the town's people's committee was restored, and people's courts proceeded to try and to execute a number of captured policemen, as well as some other government officials, landlords and people termed 'rightists'. People's committees were also restored in

A village on Cheju Island during the suppression of the insurgency.

numerous small communities and islands near Yosu. Rebel leaders told followers that the thirty-eighth parallel had been done away with and that unification with the North would soon follow.

Rhee and his American backers immediately charged that North Korea had fomented the rebellion, but it was, in fact, an outburst dating back to the frustrated goals of local leftists over the previous three years. A rebel newspaper referred to a 'three-year fight' against the American occupation and demanded that all Americans leave Korea forthwith. It announced that all agencies of government should be handed over to the Yosu people's committee and called for land redistribution without compensation to landlords, a purge of police and other officials who had served the Japanese and opposition to a separate government for the South.

The suppression of the rebellion was organized and directed by Americans and carried out by young Korean colonels, even though the occupation had ended and the USA ostensibly had no mandate to intervene in Korean internal affairs. But secret protocols placed operational control of the ROK military in American hands, and American advisers were with all ROK Army units. American C–47 transports ferried Korean troops, weapons and other *matériel*; American intelligence organizations worked closely with Army and KNP counterparts.

The revolutionary terror of the rebels left hundreds of policemen, officials and landlords dead; after the rebel defeat, loyalists predictably took their awful retribution. American sources reported that 'loyal troops were shooting people whom they had the slightest suspicion . . . of giving cooperation to the communist uprising.' James Hausman, who helped to organize the suppression, reported that police in Sunchon were 'out for revenge and are executing prisoners and civilians . . . loyal civilians already killed and people beginning to think we [*sic*] are as bad as the enemy.'

*Official estimates of casualties from the Yosu rebellion*

| | |
|---|---|
| loyalist soldiers dead: 141 | rebels killed: 821 |
| missing: 263 | rebels captured: 2,860 |
| civilians dead: 1,000+ | still guerrillas: 1,000+ |

**Korean women in Sunchon mourn relatives killed by rebels, as KMAG adviser Lt Ralph Bliss looks on. The caption in *Life*, where the photo appeared, says, 'An American adviser looks on silently where no advice will help,' but omits to mention that American officers, led by James Hausman, were directly involved in suppressing the uprising.**

Some rebels were given lenient treatment for helping to hunt down their comrades: one of these, allegedly, was Park Chung Hee, the future President. His participation in the rebellion is documented in American files; it has also been claimed that he played a role in tracking down rebels (including his own brother), but this cannot be verified. When Park made his *coup d'état* in 1961, Kennedy administration officials thought he might be a communist because of this background; adviser Roger Hilsman thought it might be the cleverest communist takeover in history.

The Yosu rebellion was a fierce tempest for a week or so, but ultimately it was a storm in a teacup, which Rhee used to clamp down upon any resistance to his rule, save that tepid and unthreatening, if none the less clamorous, dissent registered by the Democratic Party opposition. Yosu cannot be compared with the autumn uprisings in 1946 in extent and importance; it was a spontaneous and hasty mutiny by disgruntled soldiers that merely brought down more repression.

### Guerrilla Warfare in South Korea

**Arrested rebels at Sunchon, trussed and ready to be hauled away in army trucks.**

Organized guerrilla warfare on the mainland dates from November 1948, after more than a thousand Yosu rebels fled to the Chiri mountains and joined up with guerrillas and bandits already in the hills. Guerrilla strength, however, was said to 'fluctuate widely' because the activists went back and forth between their mountain bases and their villages for 'an outward resumption of normal life'.

One CIA estimate suggested that the total number of guerrillas in the South in early 1949 was somewhere between 3,500 and 6,000, not counting several thousands on Cheju. Some were armed with rifles, mostly Japanese and American, but many carried just clubs and bamboo spears. Food and other supplies came from foraging, contributions made by villages or the theft of rice stocks. American advisers thought overall strategy was in North Korean hands, passed through the Labour Party's headquarters in Haeju, just across the thirty-eighth parallel. One team of sixty guerrillas was known to have been dispatched from the North, and defectors estimated that another 1,000 or so were undergoing training for missions in the South.

The Cholla and Kyongsang provinces, the Americans said, 'have been noted for extensive leftist activities since the liberation'. Here,

> the People's Republic and its people's committees were strongest. It was in those rich, rice-producing provinces that the Japanese had most exploited the peasants. It was in those provinces that the communist-directed All Korea Farmers' Union was able to organize swiftly and, apparently, well during the first years of the American occupation.

Two Embassy vice-consuls toured the provinces in early 1949 and found that in South Cholla 'the government has lost control outside of the cities and larger towns.' Police stations in the province were 'universally protected by huge stone walls of recent construction or by high mounds of sand bags . . . Each police box resembles a medieval fort.' The authorities had carried out extensive tree cutting in the hills to deny cover to the rebels, and all travel at night was prohibited. The province's governor said there were 100,000 refugees from the guerrilla fighting in the province – many of them created by authorities who emptied villages. In North Kyongsang investigators found much ill-feeling between the police and the local populace; Taegu was tightly controlled and curfewed. Kyongju, the ancient Korean

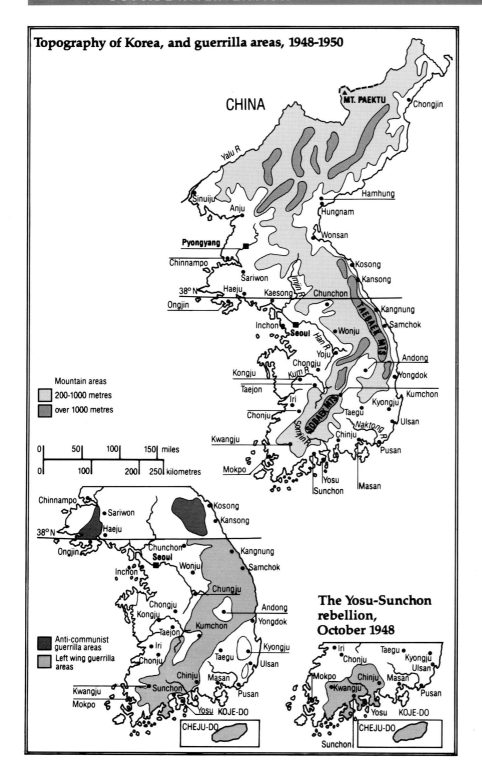

**Topography of Korea, and guerrilla areas, 1948-1950**

CHINA

MT. PAEKTU

Chongjin

Yalu R

Sinuiju

Anju

Hamhung

Hungnam

Pyongyang

Wonsan

Chinnampo

Kosong

Sariwon

Kansong

38° N

Haeju

Kaesong

Chunchon

Imjin

Ongjin

Kangnung

TAEBAEK MTS

Inchon

Seoul

Wonju

Samchok

Han R

Yoju

Chongju

Andong

Kongju

Kum R

Yongdok

Taejon

Kumchon

Iri

Kyongju

Chonju

Taegu

Ulsan

Naktong R

Sorak R

Chinju

Kwangju

Pusan

SORAK MTS

Mokpo

Yosu

Masan

Sunchon

Mountain areas
- 200-1000 metres
- over 1000 metres

| 0 | 50 | 100 | 150 | miles |
| 0 | 100 | 200 | 250 | kilometres |

Chinnampo

Kosong

Sariwon

Kansong

38° N

Haeju

Chunchon

Ongjin

Kangnung

Seoul

Wonju

Samchok

Inchon

Chungju

Chongju

Andong

Kongju

Yongdok

Taejon

Kumchon

Iri

Kyongju

Chonju

Taegu

Ulsan

Chinju

Masan

Anti-communist
guerrilla areas

Left wing guerrilla
areas

Kwangju

Sunchon

Pusan

Mokpo

Yosu

KOJE-DO

CHEJU-DO

**The Yosu-Sunchon
rebellion,
October 1948**

Iri

Taegu

Kyongju

Chonju

Ulsan

Mokpo

Chinju

Masan

Kwangju

Pusan

Yosu

KOJE-DO

CHEJU-DO

Sunchon

44

capital, was 'a mountainous area infested by communists who hide in the hills and make frequent raids on the villages'.

An American account of a survey of North Kyongsang in July 1949 related:

> Small attacks and ambushes punctuated by larger attacks characterized almost every locale. Police boxes were barricaded to the roof, trees everywhere were cut down within 100 meters of the roads, local officials and policemen felt compelled to move nervously from house to house at night.

Except in remote and under-populated places, the guerrillas were not able to hold several towns at the same time or to create base areas outside the mountains. They would enter a village at night, call out the population, give speeches and secure food and other supplies. As their situation got more desperate, especially when winter dawned in 1949, they would attack whole villages and lay them waste in search of supplies. Attacks on police stations were the most common sort of activity, both because of widespread hatred for the National Police and because records of leftist families were kept at the stations.

Walter Sullivan of *The New York Times* was almost alone among foreign journalists in seeking out the facts of this guerrilla war. Large parts of South Korea, he wrote in early 1950, 'are darkened today by a cloud of terror that is probably unparalleled in the world'. In the 'hundreds of villages across the guerrilla areas' local village guards 'crouch in pyramided

**Chief of Staff of the South Korean Army, Chae Pyong-dok (known as 'Fat Chae'), a former ordnance officer in the Japanese Imperial Army, addressing a meeting, 26 September 1949. Seated behind him are top officials in KMAG, the (US) Korean Military Advisory Group: immediately behind Chae is the head of KMAG, Brigadier-General William L. Roberts; second from right in dark shirt is Major James W. Hausman, the key US intelligence officer and *éminence grise* of the ROK Army.**

Yi Chu-gyong, an activist with the South Korean Labour Party, arrested 10 May 1948.

A Korean police station shortly after it was bombed on the day of the first National Assembly elections, 10 May 1948.

straw shelters', and nights 'are a long, cold vigil of listening'. Guerrillas made brutal assaults on police, and the police took the guerrillas to their home villages and tortured them for information. Then the police shot them, and tied them to trees as an object lesson.

The persistence of the guerrillas, Sullivan wrote, 'puzzles many Americans here', as does 'the extreme brutality' of the conflict. But Sullivan went on to argue that 'there is great divergence of wealth' in the country, with both middle and poor peasants living 'a marginal existence'. He interviewed ten peasant families; none owned all of its own land, and most were tenants. The landlord took 30 per cent of tenant produce, but additional exactions – government taxes and various contributions – ranged from 48 to 70 per cent of the annual crop.

**Members of a rightist youth group, recruited by the Korean National Police to act as vigilantes, guarding villages near Kwangju against guerrillas, May 1948.**

There was little evidence of Soviet or North Korean support for the Southern guerrillas. In April 1950 the Americans found that the North Koreans had supported guerrillas in Kangwon and along the upper coast of North Kyongsang with weapons and supplies but that 'almost 100 per cent of the guerrillas in the Cholla and Kyongsang provinces have been recruited locally'. No Soviet weapons had ever been authenticated in South Korea except near the parallel; most guerrillas had Japanese and American arms. Another report found that the guerrillas 'apparently receive little more than moral support from North Korea'.

The Edinburgh-educated chief of the Seoul Metropolitan Police, Chang Taek-sang, in 1946. He was loathed by liberal Americans in the occupation; a historian described him as having 'the face of Nero and the manners of Goering'.

The principal source of external involvement in the guerrilla war was, in fact, American. Americans usually perceive an important gap between the withdrawal of US combat forces in June 1949 and the war that came a year later, such that the question becomes: why did the Americans return? But the point is that they never left. American advisers were all over the war zones in the South, constantly shadowing their Korean counterparts and urging them to greater effort.

The man who distinguished himself in this was James Hausman, one of the key organizers of the suppression of the Yosu rebellion, who spent the next three decades as a go-between and nexus point between the American and Korean militaries and their intelligence outfits. He was a wily operator who hid his skills behind the mannerisms of an Arkansas

A rural fort manned by
counter-insurgent forces,
March 1950.

Families evacuated from
guerrilla areas by police,
March 1950.

hayseed. In an interview Hausman termed himself the father of the Korean Army, which was not far from the truth. He said that everyone knew this but could not say it publicly. In the USA hardly anyone has heard of him.

At the end of September 1949 KMAG chief Roberts said that it was of the 'utmost importance' that the guerrillas 'be cleared up as soon as possible' and asked that the US Army dispatch more infantry officers to work with the ROK Army. Every division in the ROK Army, he told MacArthur, was being diverted in part or in full from the parallel to the interior and 'ordered to exterminate guerrilla bands in their zones'.

Roberts later said that 6,000 guerrillas had been killed in the November 1949–March 1950 period, in what he called an 'all-out mop-up campaign [that] broke the backbone of the guerrilla movement'.

If the Rhee regime had one unqualified success, viewed through the American lens, it was the apparent defeat of the Southern partisans by the spring of 1950. A year before it had appeared that the guerrilla movement would only grow with the passage of time, but the suppression campaign begun in the autumn of 1949 resulted in high body counts and a perception that the guerrillas could no longer mount significant operations when the spring foliage returned in early 1950.

Both Dean Acheson and George Kennan saw the suppression of the internal threat as the litmus test for their support of the Rhee regime: if this worked, so would American-backed containment; if it did not, the regime would be viewed as another Kuomintang, as 'little China'. Colonel Goodfellow had told Rhee in late 1948, in the context of a letter in which he referred to his 'many opportunities to talk with [Acheson] about Korea', that the guerrillas had to be 'cleaned out quickly . . . everyone is watching how Korea handles the communist threat'. A weak policy would lose support in Washington; handle the threat well, and 'Korea will be held in high esteem'.

In May and June 1950 guerrilla incidents tapered off remarkably, reaching in early June a 'new low'. The last report filed before the war began said that small bands of fifteen to thirty guerrillas still operated in various areas but were generally quiet.

### The Border Fighting in 1949

The war that began in June 1950 followed on the guerrilla war and a summer of battles along the thirty-eighth parallel in 1949; this 1949 border fighting is essential to an understanding of what happened a year later. The battles began at Kaesong on 4 May 1949, in an engagement that the South started, lasting about four days and taking an official toll of 400 North Korean and twenty-two South Korean soldiers, as well as upwards of a hundred civilian deaths in Kaesong, according to American and South Korean figures. The South committed six infantry companies and several battalions, and two of the companies defected to the North.

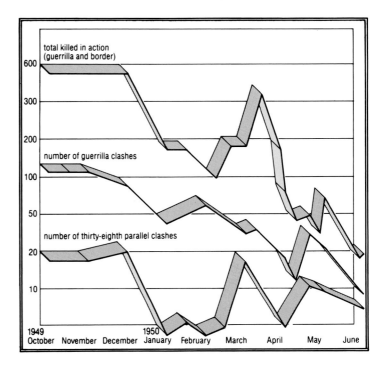

total killed in action
(guerrilla and border)

number of guerrilla clashes

number of thirty-eighth parallel clashes

**Guerrilla and thirty-eighth parallel fighting October 1949 – June 1950, based on a graph in Bruce Cumings's Introduction to Cumings (ed.),** *Child of Conflict: The Korean–American Relationship 1943–1953* **(Washington/London, University of Seattle Press, 1983), p. 39.**

Another important battle occurred on the Sunday morning of the last weekend of June 1949, on the remote Ongjin Peninsula above Seoul on the west coast. After this engagement the United Nations Commission on Korea (UNCOK) sent a delegation to investigate; it arrived courtesy of a South Korean naval vessel and was guided around by ROK Army personnel. United Nations observers remained at Ongjin for a day or so and returned to Seoul on Monday evening; they then filed a report to the UN blaming 'northern invaders' for the trouble. It is likely that the North was to blame for this one, but what is remarkable is the utter failure of UN observers to investigate and report upon the many battles started by the South as well.

The worst fighting of 1949 occurred in early August, when North Korean forces attacked ROK Army units occupying a small mountain north of the thirty-eighth parallel. It went on for days, right through an important conference between Syngman Rhee and Chiang Kai-shek.

Ambassador Muccio penned two long memoranda after this fighting, which deserve quotation nearly in full:

> Captain Shin stated that the reports from Ongjin reaching military headquarters on the morning of August 4 were most alarming. These reports indicated that the [South] Korean forces on the [Ongjin] peninsula had been completely routed and that there was nothing there to stand against the northern onslaught. He went on that in studying the situation with the general staff . . . the military were insistent that the only way to relieve pressure on Ongjin

would be to drive north. The military urged mounting an immediate attack north towards Charwon [Cholwon].

In line with the advice given by General Roberts, Captain Shin decided against attack and took immediate steps to send limited reinforcements into Ongjin.

Captain Shin went on that as soon as the Prime Minister [Yi Pom-sok] returned from the Rhee–Chiang meeting . . . he called Captain Shin and remonstrated with him that he should have had more courage, should have attacked the North. That General Lee [Pom-sok] took this position does not surprise me especially. It did surprise me, however, when Captain Shin went on to say that upon his return from Chinhae the following day President Rhee also told him that he should not have decided against attacking Charwon.

On 16 August Muccio went on to relate that Rhee, in a conversation with Muccio,

threw out the thought that . . . he might replace [Chief of Staff] Chae [Pyong-dok] with General Kim Suk Wan [Kim Sok-won] . . . Kim Suk Wan has long been a favorite of President Rhee. Last fall prior to Yosu Rhee mentioned to General Coulter and myself that Kim had offered to 'take care of the North' if he could be supplied with 20,000 rifles for Korean veterans of the Japanese Army who were burning with patriotism. The Minister of Defense, the Korean general staff and American advisers are all against General Kim. They do not consider him a good soldier but a blusterer. They have called my attention to his propensity for needling northern forces in his sector of the front, for resorting to Japanese banzai attacks and for deploying all his forces in a most hazardous manner right on the front without adequate reserves. They particularly object to his ignoring headquarters and going direct to President Rhee.

**Syngman Rhee, *centre*, meets Chiang Kai-shek (on Rhee's immediate right) and his entourage in the southern naval port of Chinhae, August 1949. Madame Rhee is on Chiang's right.**

General Roberts did indeed order Southern commanders not to attack and threatened to remove American advisers if they did; British sources said that ROK Army commanders' heads were 'full of ideas of recovering the North by conquest. Only the American Ambassador's stern warning that all American aid would be stopped . . . prevented the Army from attempting to attack across the parallel at another point when the communists attacked at Ongjin.'

Although an attack in early August was aborted, by the end of the month Muccio described the situation as follows:

> There is increasing confidence in the Army. An aggressive, offensive spirit is emerging. Nerves that were frayed and jittery the past few months may now give way to this new spirit. A good portion of the Army is eager to get going. More and more people feel that the only way unification can be brought about is by moving north by force. I have it from Dick Johnston [a *New York Times* reporter] that Chiang Kai-shek told Rhee that the Nationalist air force could support a move north and that they discussed the possibility of the Nationalists starting an offensive move against Manchuria through Korea! There is some feeling that now is the time to move north while the Chinese communists are preoccupied. I doubt whether Rhee would actually order a move north in his saner moments. Captain Shin, I know, is dead against it. Lee Bum Suk [Yi Pom-sok] would love it. However, should we have another Kaesong or Ongjin flare-up, a counter-attack might lead to all sorts of unpredictable developments.

**Kim Sok-won with an unidentified American planning fighting, summer 1949.**

**Colonel Paek In-yop,** *second right*, **Commander of the ROK 17th Regiment, on the Ongjin peninsula immediately prior to 25 June 1950 (see p. 71). The caption to this agency still says Colonel Paek is 'in consultation at Ongjin during one of the guerrilla skirmishes that preceded the [25 June] invasion'.**

On 23 August the ROK sent several naval patrol boats right up the Taedong river to Mongumpo, sinking four North Korean ships of 35- to 45-ton class; Inchon harbour was reinforced in case of a counter-attack (which did not eventuate). At the end of September Rhee again made clear his desire to march north. In a letter of 30 September 1949 from Rhee to Oliver (the authenticity of which the USA denied during UN debates in the autumn of 1950 but which Dr Oliver verified as valid), Rhee said:

> I feel strongly that now is the most psychological moment when we should take an aggressive measure and join with our loyal communist army [sic] in the North to clear up the rest of them in Pyongyang. We will drive some of Kim Il Sung's men to the mountain region and there we will gradually starve them out. Then our line of defense must be strengthened along the Tuman and Yalu rivers [i.e., the Sino-Korean border].

The point is not that North Korea was an innocent party to this fighting but that both sides were at fault – and, according to several statements by Roberts, the South started more of the battles than did the North. Also important is the opening of the fighting in the Ongjin and Kaesong areas in many of the 1949 battles, for this is where the war began a year later. A tantalizing detail is that after ROK defences collapsed at Ongjin in early August, ROK commanders considered both an attack north against Chorwon *and* a very rapid pull-back – perhaps all the way to an offshore island.

The veteran journalist A. T. Steele captured the flavour of all this in a remarkable account written in October 1949: 'An unadmitted shooting war between the governments of the US and Russia is in effect today along the thirty-eighth parallel. . . . It is smoldering throughout the territory of the new Republic of Korea . . . only American money, weapons, and technical assistance enable [the Republic] to exist for more than a few hours'. The ROK was 'dedicated to liberty', Steele wrote, but it was 'a tight little dictatorship run as a police state'. Its jails overflowed with prisoners – 30,000 according to his estimate; 'torture of captured political antagonists is commonplace'; and 'women and children are killed without compunction' by both sides. Americans on the scene were 'almost evangelical in their fervor for Korean revival', but, Steele thought, 'once the American props are withdrawn, South Korea will fall beneath the weight of communist Asia'.

Leaders gather for the founding of the DPRK. Kim Il Sung is flanked on his left by Pak Hon-yong, Hong Myong-hi, Choe Yong-gon, Pak Il-u, Yi Sung-yop and Kim Won-bong, with an unidentified man on the far right; to Kim's right is Kim Chaek, with Mu Jong – a famous Yenan-aligned commander – visible between them in the next row.

## North Korea

Little was known about North Korea in the 1940s; it was always assumed that the USSR ruled the roost. Recent studies indicate that the main points about North Korea were: first, that it had evolved an indigenous political system in the late 1940s, and its basic structure has not changed substantially; second, that Soviet influence was always in competition with Chinese influence in Korea, and both were in conflict with indigenous

Elections to form the ▷
Democratic People's
Republic of Korea, August
1948. The banner reads,
'For the sake of our rich
and strong Democratic
People's Republic!'

political forms and practices; third, the closest comparison with North Korea
was Yugoslavia, not the states under complete Soviet hegemony such as East
Germany. The DPRK was, and is, a divergent case among established
Marxist–Leninist systems, representing a profound reassertion of native
Korean political practice – from the superordinate role of the leader, to his
self-reliant ideology, to the independent foreign-policy stance.

R. S. Milward of the British Foreign Office wrote in mid-1948
that North Korea had

> an apparent similarity to the more autonomous western commu-
> nist states such as Yugoslavia. Kim Il Sung . . . was built up during
> the war into an almost legendary guerrilla hero . . . a Korean Tito.
> The Russians moreover are proposing to withdraw their forces
> from Korea, seeming to trust their puppets . . . [to] rule the land in
> the interests of Russia without direct Russian interference.

55

Kim Il Sung passes out the first domestically produced machine guns to top commanders of the People's Army: *left to right*, Choe Yong-gon, Kim Chaek and Kim Il, *c.* 1948.

This 'façade of autonomy', Milward thought, was more pronounced than in 'almost any other country in the Russian orbit'. The internal contradiction in this report (that North Korea was similar to Yugoslavia, yet was a puppet that would rule in Moscow's interests) probably reflected both a general Western inability to believe that Koreans could be independent, and lack of experience, at that point, with communist regimes that had directly defied Moscow.

A CIA study one year later made sharp distinctions between the Euro-Mediterranean region and East Asia, citing 'a generally detached attitude' towards communism in East Asia in 1945–9. The Soviet looting of Manchuria, the CIA thought, suggested that the USSR did not want to build a dependent economic complex and had problems controlling Asian nationalism and 'Titoism'.

North Korea was never simply a Soviet satellite in the 1940s but evolved from a coalition regime based on widespread 'people's committees' in 1945–6 to a period of relative Soviet dominance in 1947–8, thence in 1949 to important links with China, which in turn provided the DPRK with scope to manoeuvre between the two communist giants. Kim Il Sung was not a hand-picked Soviet puppet but organized politically first to establish his leadership, then to isolate and best the communists who had remained in Korea during the colonial period, then to ally with Soviet-aligned Koreans for a time, then to create under his own leadership (in February 1948) a powerful army that welded Koreans who had fought together in Manchuria and China proper with those who remained at home.

That army was the backbone of Kim's dominance. Its leaders were hard-bitten guerrillas with as much as twenty years' experience. As the civil war grew in China, these men came to command tens of thousands of soldiers. The Communist or Workers' Party had a social base in the vast peasantry, with an inner circle constituted by the Kim Il Sung group. This group used the party apparatus to recruit a mass base for Kim's rule, an open-door policy in which almost anyone could be a party member, regardless of class background, and which brought masses of poor peasants into the party ranks. Instead of a vanguard party comprising 2 or 3 per cent of the population, North Korea had a party encompassing 12 to 14 per cent, meaning perhaps a quarter or more of the entire adult population.

Even among party leaders, poor peasant background was common. In a secret compilation of data on some 1,881 'cultural cadres' in late 1949, 66 per cent came from poor peasant backgrounds, 19 per cent from proletarian backgrounds. Fully 422 of these cadres had experience in the Chinese Eighth Route Army.

The greatest divergence in North Korean socialism came at the commanding heights of the regime, the core leadership that constituted the real vanguard of the revolution. The organizational principle here was personal loyalty among a tightly knit inner circle, which then became the nucleus of ever-widening concentric circles. The bond holding that core together was based on the prestige of the personalities who had fought in the guerrilla struggle against Japan.

In 1946 and 1947 the North Koreans eliminated all non-leftist political opposition with remarkable thoroughness. A couple of 'united front' non-communist parties were allowed to exist, but they had no power. The intent was the same as that of the right wing in the South, to squash alternative centres of power. But the Northerners did it much more effectively because of their superior organization and the general weakness of the opposition. Neither North nor South had qualms about using violence towards political ends, but the North tended to be more discriminating, in part because its enemies were numerically small classes and groups, and also because of a political practice, perhaps growing out of the Korean leadership's experience with Chinese communism, of seeking to re-educate and reform political recalcitrants.

Christians were a particular target. Christianity took hold in Korea in a way that it did not in Japan or China, and even if the number of believers in the general population was not more than 2 per cent in 1945, they were numerous and influential in Pyongyang. American sources thought that Christian Churches formed the strongest opposition to the regime, and scattered evidence suggests that many pastors were imprisoned in the late 1940s, including the Reverend Sun Myung Moon, who ran a sect called the Israel Church and who was imprisoned on charges of fornication and adultery in 1948 and 1949. In one particularly bloody incident police fired on a crowd of Christian protesters in Sinuiju, killing twenty-three people; Ham Sok-hon, the famous Quaker human rights figure, was then in the provincial

58

**May 1948: US Signal Corps caption reads: 'Informal picture of Dr Rhee Syngman, number one rightist leader of Korea and the only standout of importance against communism in the nation.'**

**Kim Jong Il, son and successor to Kim Il Sung, c. 1947.**

people's committee, but he was beaten and arrested after this incident. Kim Il Sung personally visited Sinuiju, seeking to mend rifts between communists and Christian nationalists. Christian churches remained open until the war, and worship was allowed, but Christian political activities were stamped out.

The regime did not engage in massive slaughter of its enemies, however, such as those carried out in the USSR in the early 1930s or in China and Vietnam in their violent land-reform campaigns. Landlords were allowed to flee south or work small plots of land, and leadership purges before the war were usually neither fatal nor permanent.

Press freedom ceased to exist in the North; all newspapers – central and local, communist and non-communist – carried essentially the same news, with some local colouring thrown in. Furthermore, Soviet-aligned Koreans tended to predominate in the cultural organs; all three of the editors of the party journal were 'Soviet-Koreans' (usually meaning Koreans who had lived in the USSR or followed the Soviet lead) in 1945–50.

The security apparatus was very large in the North. Its functions included a system of thought control and surveillance; the regime organized secret networks on a grand scale to report political statements, including rumours and hearsay, as a means both of checking on citizen loyalty and of providing the leadership with a rudimentary guide to public opinion.

For years many have speculated that if the USSR did not control Korea, the 'Soviet-Koreans' did. A retrospective State Department study asserted that a group of some forty-three Koreans who were born in or resided in the Soviet Union, most of whom were members of the Communist Party in 1945, constituted the core of the Soviet-Korean group; but even according to this official account, they played only 'secondary roles' until after the Korean war, with Kim Il Sung's main competition coming from native communists and China-aligned groups. Although the Soviet-Koreans' power increased briefly in the early 1950s, they were 'virtually eliminated' by 1956, according to this study. The head of this group was Ho Ka-i, a proponent of Soviet models of organization described as 'a disciplinarian in the best Bolshevik tradition', working closely with the Soviet Embassy. The CIA put great emphasis on Ho Ka-i, viewing him as a key liaison between the Soviets and the Koreans and, according to hearsay evidence, an 'enormous' behind-the-scenes influence.

Recent careful work suggests a different picture. The leading scholar on Soviet–Korean relations, Professor Haruki Wada, found that among Stalin's large grouping of international communists in Moscow, not a single Korean communist or nationalist existed who was clearly 'a trusted Soviet man'. In 1937 Stalin ordered the forced deportation of some 200,000 Koreans from the Soviet Far East to Central Asia, on the racist grounds that they might harbour pro-Japanese seditious elements. 'At the same time all Korean communists who were working in the Comintern were arrested and killed as [potential] agents of Japanese militarism.' Professor Wada also suggested that the Soviets may have subjected Kim Il Sung and other Korean guerrillas to investigation and interrogation when they moved back and forth across the Soviet–Manchurian border in the 1940s, keeping them under surveillance for a long time. In extant Soviet studies of Manchuria under the Japanese, Kim Il Sung is usually not mentioned – distinctly short shrift for an alleged Soviet puppet.

The number of Soviet advisers was never very high in the North, even in the military. British sources estimated that Soviet advisers to the central government dropped from 200 in 1946 to only thirty in April 1947, the greatest number of those, predictably, being in the Ministry of the Interior. Soviet Colonel G. K. Plotnikov told us that between 200 and 250 Soviet advisers were left behind after the Red Army pulled out. The South Korean Defence Minister put the number of Soviet military advisers at only 120 before the war, which accords with intelligence estimates after the war began, saying the Soviets used 'approximately fifteen advisory officers per [North Korean] division', there being fewer than ten divisions before June 1950. There were only fifteen Soviet advisers to the Korean Air Force. Advisers went down to the battalion level, the Americans liked to say, which sounds impressive. But there were three regiments to each division and three battalions to each regiment. If the total number were around 120, fifteen per division, then a battalion would have had only one or two Soviet advisers. This Soviet presence simply cannot be compared with fully functioning satellites in Eastern Europe, which had thousands of Soviet staff people and advisers.

It has been asserted that the USSR provided North Korea with vast amounts of weaponry just before the war. The North did get a great deal of World War II vintage tanks, artillery and planes, although most of them had been left when Soviet forces departed in 1948. There is little evidence of the shipment of new equipment in 1950. Within weeks of the opening of the fighting in June the CIA reported that the North's equipment 'appears to have been obsolete or obsolescent Soviet discards'. Hanson Baldwin reported at about the same time that the North had nothing beyond World War II vintage equipment. Military historians later concluded that the USSR had been reluctant to equip the North with its newer weaponry, even during the worst periods of the war, let alone before the war. The new Stalin tank, the heavy 152-mm howitzer and other advanced weaponry were never supplied, which 'lessened the effectiveness of the North Korean enemy immeasurably'. The Soviets also *sold* their weaponry to the North before and through much of the war; they even exacted payment for the large stocks of equipment they left behind in 1948. One glaring difference between the South and North was in air capability, the North having propeller-driven fighters and light bombers. All of these planes were of pre-1945 vintage, however, with no jet aircraft such as the USSR delivered to the Chinese in the spring of 1950.

In late February 1949 Kim Il Sung left Pyongyang for his only official visit to the Soviet Union before the Korean war. When he returned to Korea in March, Kim brought with him an economic and cultural agreement and, intelligence rumour had it, a secret military agreement. We do not know

Kim Il Sung departing for Moscow on his only known visit before the Korean war, late February 1949. *From left:* Pak Hon-yong, Foreign Minister (and leader of the South Korean communists); Ho Hon, a leading figure in the 1945 People's Republic set up in Seoul in 1945; Terentyi Shtykov, Soviet Ambassador; unidentified; Kim Il Sung; Kim Tu-bong, who headed the Communist Party in the North in the initial period after the Japanese surrender and later became state President.

much about what was discussed at these talks. It seems unthinkable that Kim did not discuss the question of unification. In the West it is generally asserted that Stalin colluded with Kim about starting a war. The heavily edited Khruschchev memoirs claim that Kim returned to Moscow once between March 1949 and June 1950 to discuss the matter, although there is no good evidence that this is true. The USSR made the Koreans pay for everything, including a 220-million-rouble loan at 2 per cent interest, which was about what mortgages returned to American banks in 1949 – that is, there was profit in it. At this time South Korea was getting more than $100 million a year from the USA, most of it in the form of outright grants. The entire Southern national budget for 1951 was $120 million, with $27 million earmarked for defence, and American aid for the year 1951 was set at $100 million.

## North Korea and China

Even before the entry of Chinese forces into the Korean war China had an important influence on the North – mainly through tens of thousands of Koreans who fought in the Chinese civil war, establishing a reciprocal call on Chinese assistance later on.

American intelligence paid close attention to troop and *matériel* movements across the Sino-Korean border in early 1947; North Korean military forces had expanded rapidly in late 1946 within Korea, preparing for a spring offensive in Manchuria. Some 30,000 Koreans, under the command of Kim Chaek, reportedly moved into Manchuria during April 1947; by May of that year 15 to 20 per cent of Chinese communist forces in Manchuria were

Koreans. From that point onward, until the winter of 1950, American intelligence designated these 'Chinese Communist Forces' (CCF) or 'CCF Koreans', which made it hard to identify truly Chinese soldiers when they entered the Korean war.

Several intelligence sources put the total for all Koreans in the Chinese Fourth Field Army alone at 145,000; this army, under Lin Biao, was the crack force of the communists, having never lost a battle as it swept southwards from Manchuria. Chinese Nationalist estimates were that 50,000 Koreans fought below the Great Wall. Probably the total number of Koreans who fought in China was about 100,000.

### The Eve of the War

American influence in the South had reached new heights by 1950. British Minister Vyvyan Holt eloquently captured this a few weeks before the war broke out: 'Radiating from the huge ten-storeyed Banto Hotel', American influence 'penetrates into every branch of administration and is fortified by an immense outpouring of money'. Americans kept the government, the Army, the economy, the railways, the airports, the mines and factories going, supplying money, electricity, expertise and psychological succour. American petrol fuelled every motor vehicle in the country. American cultural influence was 'exceedingly strong', ranging from scholarships to study in the USA, several strong missionary denominations, 'a score of traveling cinemas' and theatres that played mostly American films and the Voice of America, to big-league baseball: America was the 'dream-land' to thousands, if not millions, of Koreans.

The ECA and KMAG missions were the biggest of their type in the world. The US Information Service had, according to its own testimony, 'one of the most extensive country programs that we are operating anywhere', with nine centres in Korea, parlaying libraries, mobile units, a variety of publications and films. American officials ran Kimpo International Airport and controlled the entry and exit of American citizens. Besides the official presence, private Americans often advised or directed private industry.

KMAG's work in training the South's Army also seemed highly successful. In some exuberant interviews with Marguerite Higgins just before the war Roberts said, 'KMAG is a living demonstration of how an intelligent and intensive investment of 500 combat-hardened American men and officers can train 100,000 guys to do the shooting for you.' The countryside had been 'in a perpetual uproar' until recently, he said, but was now under control, thanks to American advisers 'at every level' who 'live right there with [the Koreans] . . . and stay with them in battles'. Higgins cited rumours that French counter-insurgency officers had arrived to learn about KMAG techniques for 'export' to Indochina. In sum, Roberts said, 'the American taxpayer has an army that is a fine watchdog over the investments

Liu Yu-wan, the Kuomintang Chinese delegate on the UN Commission for Korea (UNCOK) *right*, Taejon, July 1950. Liu played a key role in the Commission. *Left:* Colonel Alfred G. Katzin of South Africa, the personal representative in Korea of UN Secretary General Trygve Lie; *centre:* Australian delegate to UNCOK A. B. Jamieson; *standing:* George Movshon of the UN Secretariat.

placed in this country and a force that represents the maximum results at minimum cost.' He discounted threats about an invasion from the North, saying, 'at this point we rather invite it. It will give us target practice.'

The UN Commission on Korea barely functioned in late 1949 and early 1950. In September 1949 most of its delegates departed, virtually closing up shop. Remaining UNCOK functionaries, of which there were few, complained of their 'enforced idleness'; an Embassy memorandum of January 1950 referred contemptuously to the 'comatose Commission'. February brought hopes of a 'rejuvenated' group, and in March it was announced that military observers would be added to UNCOK, but by the end of March it was again said to be 'largely inactive'.

The delegate from Nationalist China was Liu Yu-wan, an important and trusted diplomat and the most active member of UNCOK in 1949–50. He served as its rapporteur in the autumn of 1949 and was scheduled to be chairman during the writing of UNCOK's report on the important elections on 30 May 1950 – which greatly pleased the American Embassy, since it ensured a favourable report, and also happened to place him in a key position when the war broke out.

Two UNCOK military observers completed a survey of the parallel on the afternoon of 23 June. They reported this to UNCOK on

Friday and set about 'the shaping up of the report' on Saturday, not out of a sense of urgency but because it was 'something nice and tangible' to do on a lazy weekend.

The observers slept mainly in Seoul and went up to the parallel on nine of the days between 9 and 23 June. (How much could they really see in that period? The terrain is extremely mountainous; deep valleys are cut off from each other.) They returned to Seoul from the parallel on 17 June and stayed in the city until the 21st. But from the 21st to the morning of Friday, 23 June they were on the Ongjin Peninsula, which is where the war began on the Sunday.

British sources in the spring of 1950 indicated that KMAG advisers were 'seeking the removal of over-aggressive officers in command positions along the parallel'; in the interim until they were removed, the report said, 'a border incident . . . could precipitate civil war'. The British thought that this would not happen as long as American officers controlled the situation. This lends significance to the absence of General Roberts, Colonel Wright and other highly placed KMAG officers in late June 1950. Roberts was on his way home to retirement, and Wright was in Tokyo.

On 30 May 1950, a few weeks before the war began, the South held its second National Assembly elections. The result was a disastrous loss for the Rhee regime, bringing into the Assembly a strong collection of moderates, several of them associated with Yo Un-hyong's political lineage and most of them hoping for peaceful unification with the North. The Korean Ambassador to the USA, John Chang, informed American officials of a crisis in his regime in early June, prompting John Foster Dulles to decide to visit Korea on his way to see MacArthur in Tokyo.

**The UN Field Observers, Wing Commander Ronald J. Rankin and Colonel F. S. B. Peach, with secretary Charles Coates, *centre*, being welcomed at Pupo-ri on the Ongjin Peninsula, 22 June 1950.**

In Tokyo MacArthur hoped for a change in US policy in the Far East, especially with regard to Taiwan. On Taiwan Chiang hoped the talks with MacArthur would herald a commitment to his regime. In Seoul Rhee hoped for a military alliance with the USA. In Pyongyang Dulles's longstanding pro-Japan position would raise the gravest suspicions.

During Dulles's visit to Seoul Rhee not only pushed for a direct American defence but also advocated an attack on the North. Dulles invited along with him a favourite reporter, William Mathews, editor of the *Arizona Daily Star*. Mathews wrote just after the meeting between Rhee and Dulles: 'He is militantly for the unification of Korea. Openly says it must be brought about soon . . . Rhee pleads justice of going into North country. Thinks it could succeed in a few days . . . if he can do it with our help, he will do it.' And Mathews noted that Rhee said he would 'do it', 'even if it brought on a general war'. All this was yet more proof of Rhee's provocative behaviour, but it was no different from his threats to march north made many times before. The Dulles visit was vintage Rhee, but there is little evidence that Dulles was in collusion with him, as the North Koreans have always claimed.

**An agency photograph dated 28 June 1950 and titled 'North Korean women guerrillas captured at border; first pictures of Korean struggle'. The text says that the photo shows 'North Korean women guerrillas, one of whom is carrying a baby, who were captured by South Korean soldiers near the border a few days before the invasion and placed in custody in a stockade'.**

After the Korean war Herbert Feis questioned Dean Acheson about Dulles's visit: 'Are you sure his presence didn't provoke the attack, Dean? There has been comment about that – I don't think it did. You have no views on the subject?'

Acheson's response was deadpan: 'No, I have no views on the subject.'

George Kennan then interjected: 'There is a comical aspect to this, because the visits of these people over there, and their peering over outposts with binoculars at the Soviet people, I think must have led the Soviets to think that we were on to their plan and caused them considerable perturbation.'

'Yes,' Acheson said. 'Foster up in a bunker with a homburg on – it was a very amusing picture.'

It may be, however, that Chinese Nationalists on Taiwan were willing to intrigue with Rhee. From the New Year onwards American and British intelligence agencies predicted that the 'last battle' of the Chinese civil war would come in June 1950. In January British Foreign Office sources predicted an invasion of Taiwan 'by the end of June'. Guy Burgess, interestingly enough, watched this situation closely. In April Burgess said the invasion would come in May/June or September/October.

In the autumn of 1949 William Pawley, Charles Cooke and other Americans had organized an 'informal' military advisory group to

US special envoy John Foster Dulles at the thirty-eighth parallel, 17 June 1950. ROK Chief of Staff Chae, *top left*; ROK Minister of Defence Shin Sung-mo in pith helmet; ROK Foreign Minister Ben Limb in straw hat behind Shin.

help with the defence of Taiwan. Pawley later became a key CIA operative, influential in the overthrow of the Arbenz regime in Guatemala and in the Bay of Pigs adventure. Pawley and Cooke operated outside the established channels of American foreign policy, seeking to retrieve Chiang and his regime from their impending demise.

**Nationalist Chinese Generals Ho Ying-chen,** *left,* **and Sun Li-jen. Sun, educated at Virginia Military Institute, was an American favourite and candidate to replace Chiang Kai-shek in planning for a** *coup d'état* **as the Korean war began.**

Chiang Kai-shek also faced maturing plans by American clandestine officers for a *coup d'état* against him, a fact that has long been shrouded in secrecy. Like the Rhee regime, the Chiang regime was gravely at risk in June 1950. In May the Nationalists appeared to be played out. Even American partisans of Chiang's regime seemed to draw back after the Nationalists failed to defend Hainan Island. Intelligence estimates continued to predict an invasion in June; the American consul, Robert Strong, reported from Taipei on 17 May, 'Fate of Taiwan sealed, communist attack can occur between June 15 and end July.' The next day the Taipei consulate said that the best guess from a meeting of all American representatives was that the island would be attacked before 15 July.

Dean Rusk told us in an interview that some elements of the Nationalist military were preparing to move against Chiang, but then the Korean war intervened. Just after the war began, Kennan told a top-secret National Security Council meeting that there was a possibility that 'Chiang might be overthrown at any time'.

67

Guy Burgess in London read everything coming in from Taiwan in May and June 1950, including unclassified press reports. The British chancery in Moscow had earlier noted that Soviet newspapers took an inordinate interest in any scraps of information on the Taiwan question. Burgess's judgement on 24 June 1950 was that 'the Soviets seem to have made up their minds that the USA have a finally decided policy [not to defend Taiwan]. This *we* [*sic*] have never quite come to believe.'

With all this bubbling activity, the last weekend in June 1950 none the less dawned on a torpid, somnolent and very empty Washington. Harry Truman was back home in Independence. Acheson was at his Sandy Spring country farm; Kennan had disappeared to a remote summer cottage without so much as a telephone; Paul Nitze was away; the Joint Chiefs were occupied elsewhere. Even the United Nations representative, Warren Austin, was not at his post.

If we assume that all those on the 'free world' side were innocent of anything other than weekend relaxation, three well-positioned observers might yet have warned those whom they served to be on the alert – for a *coup* against Chiang, an invasion of Taiwan or trouble along the parallel in Korea. These were Guy Burgess at the Foreign Office in London, Kim Philby in Washington and George Blake, who then was the MI6 station chief in Seoul.

**The communist camp was well informed about Western policy on Korea through a group of well-placed spies.**

**Tom Driberg, *left*, and Guy Burgess outside the Sovietskaya Hotel, Moscow, 1956. Driberg, a Labour Member of Parliament, is the mystery man of the Korean war. He worked for both British and Soviet Intelligence. He was by far the best-informed MP about Korea, which he visited in late summer 1950, touring UN positions as a newspaper correspondent. He then landed behind North Korean lines with British commandos (making a pass at 'a couple of the lads' on the way, according to one participant), ignoring a three-line whip to return to the Commons. He played a key role in organizing Blake's escape from prison in 1966. Burgess was monitoring Far East events in the Foreign Office, with an eagle eye, in the period leading up to June 1950.**

Kim Philby, *centre*, and George Blake, *right*, with their Russian wives, outside Moscow. Blake was chief of British Intelligence in Seoul before the Korean war and spent the war in North Korean hands as a prisoner. Official Western opinion suggests that he was 'turned' in captivity, though this is questionable. Blake returned to British Intelligence after the Korean war, was subsequently arrested and was sentenced to forty-two years in prison in 1961. In 1966 he escaped to the USSR. Philby was British Intelligence liaison officer in Washington with the CIA at the time that the Korean war started. In 1949 he played a central role in tipping off the communist camp to the West's plans to invade Albania.

# THE WAR BEGINS

Most accounts of the outbreak of fighting in June 1950 give the impression that an attack began all along the parallel at dawn, against an enemy taken completely unawares. But the war began in the same remote locus as much of the 1949 fighting, the Ongjin Peninsula, and, some hours later, spread along the parallel eastwards, to Kaesong, Chunchon and the east coast. As an official American history put it: 'On the Ongjin Peninsula, cut off from the rest of South Korea, soldiers of the 17th Regiment stood watch on the quiet summer night of 24–25 June 1950. For more than a week, there had been no serious incident along the 38th parallel. . . . Then at 0400, with devastating suddenness . . . [artillery and mortar fire] crashed into the ROK lines.'

The North's official radio had a different account. On 26 June it said that South Korean forces had begun shelling the Unpa-san area on the Ongjin Peninsula on 23 June at 10 p.m. and had continued until 4 a.m. on 24 June, using howitzers and mortars. A Northern unit was defending Turak Mountain on Ongjin in the early hours of 25 June when it was attacked by the 'Fierce Tiger' unit of the ROK's 17th Regiment, which it proceeded to destroy. By 2.30 p.m. on 25 June the unit had advanced as far as Sudong on the Ongjin Peninsula; meanwhile partisans sprang forward to disrupt South Korean police stations and units in Ongjin.

South Korean sources asserted, on the contrary, that elements of the 17th Regiment had counter-attacked and were in possession of Haeju city, the only important point north of the thirty-eighth parallel claimed to have been taken by the South's army. This was announced at 11 o'clock on the morning of 26 June, a timing that would account for numerous newspaper articles saying that elements of the ROK Army had occupied Haeju, which have been used since to support the argument that the South might have attacked first.

The 17th Regiment was not just another unit of the ROK Army. It was directly commanded by Paek In-yop, one of two brothers who headed the North-west or *Sobuk* faction in the Army and who had been responsible for bringing many North-west Youth members into it; the other brother commanded the ROK Army's 1st Division. Both were crack units. Regional loyalties structured most units of the Army, and this one was full of Northerners with a virulent hatred of communism.

Also with the 17th was the infamous 'Tiger Kim' – from

South Korean political prisoners, Pusan, summer 1950 (see James Cameron's description, p. 92).

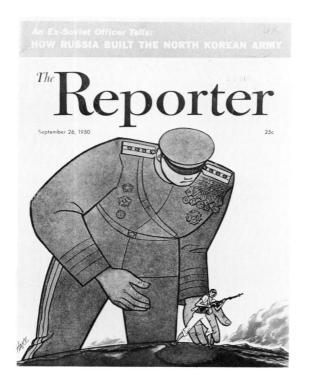

This cover of the US liberal magazine the *Reporter* shows a huge Soviet officer pushing a Korean into the flames of war. The caption reads: 'An Ex-Soviet Officer Tells: How Russia Built the North Korean Army'. The article was a CIA plant. The author, 'Colonel Kalinov', was invented. This article is often quoted in Western texts as a reliable source for a putative Russian role in the start of the war.

whence came the name *Maengho* or 'Fierce Tiger' unit – Kim Chong-won, who had got the name 'Tiger' for his services to the Japanese Army. (After 1945 he liked journalists to call him 'the Tiger of Mount Paektu', after the highest mountain in Korea.) He had volunteered for the Imperial Army in 1940, had risen to the rank of sergeant, 'a rank that epitomized the brutality of the Japanese Army at its worst', in the words of US Ambassador Muccio, and had later been one of the commanders of the suppression of the Yosu rebellion.

Fighting began at Ongjin around 3 or 4 a.m. on 25 June and had begun rippling eastward across the parallel by 5 a.m. Kaesong was the only point on the parallel where an American officer was present that morning. Joseph Darrigo, adviser to the ROK 12th Regiment, was just below Songak-san, a small mountain cleft by the thirty-eighth parallel on the north-east edge of the town, the peak of which was occupied by North Korean units. At 5 a.m. artillery fire jounced him out of bed; he hopped into a jeep and headed south towards an ROK military base near Kaesong, as he had done on many other mornings. Darrigo later reported that 'the volume of fire indicated an enemy attack' – in other words, he did not know whose artillery he heard when he awakened (in a KMAG compound, not with front-line units) at 5 a.m. An American missionary heard both the artillery and Darrigo's jeep as it went by his home, but both were such common occurrences that he rolled over and went back to sleep. Darrigo witnessed no enemy troops until he saw North Korean units disembarking at the railway station in the centre of town. The missionary woke up to find Korean People's Army (KPA) soldiers peering in his window. The 13th and 15th Regiments of the 6th KPA Division had opened their main attack at 5.30, and the town had fallen by 9.30 a.m., with almost no resistance.

At the border town of Chunchon, east of Kaesong, the South Koreans unquestionably had advance knowledge of fighting to begin on 25 June, which Southern and American sources say, of course, was advance knowledge of the North Korean attack. Thomas D. McPhail, an American intelligence officer, had amassed 'a wealth of information' from South Korean agents whom he had sent into Northern territory. On Thursday, 22 June, this information prompted him to go to Seoul, from his position near Chunchon, to warn US intelligence officials that the North had moved citizens away from the parallel and had secreted camouflaged tanks and artillery in the 'restricted area' (which must refer to the area just north of the parallel). McPhail's information caused the 6th Division commander to cancel all passes and 'fully man defensive positions for the weekend'. Because of this 'preparedness', 'the initial attack was repulsed'.

On the east coast the South's 8th Division also gave a good account of itself. But the decisive assault, according to military historian Appleman, was when Northern forces south of Chorwon at the parallel attacked the 1st Regiment of the ROK Army's 7th Division, dealing it heavy casualties; it gave way, and at some unspecified later point the 3rd and 4th KPA Divisions, with an armoured brigade, crashed through and began a daunting march south towards Seoul.

MacArthur's command reported through the UN at the end of July that the North attacked at the eastern and western portions of the parallel with reinforced border Constabulary brigades, at Kaesong and Chunchon with a division each (but, interestingly, not at the start) and ran through the Uijongbu corridor with 8,000 to 10,000 troops and fifty tanks – in other words, a total force of about 38,000. Just before the war the North Korean order of battle numbered about 95,000 troops. Thus the initial attacking force was not very large; the KPA had mobilized less than half its forces on 25 June. Arrayed against them were five ROK Army divisions located near Seoul or north of it, some 50,000 troops.

This evidence is compatible both with an unprovoked invasion and with an interpretation linking the summer of 1949 with June 1950 – that the North waited until it had the majority of its crack soldiers back from China and then positioned them to take advantage of the first major Southern provocation in June 1950.

The American position has always been that the North Koreans stealthily prepared an attack that was completely unprovoked and that constituted an all-out invasion. On 26 June Kim Il Sung, on the contrary, accused the South of making a 'general attack' across the parallel. Rhee had long sought to 'provoke' a fratricidal civil war, he said, having incessantly provoked clashes' at the front line; in preparing a 'northern expedition' he had 'even gone so far as to collude with our sworn enemy,

Japanese militarism'. Some of these charges were true, but the charge of making a general attack across the parallel is false. The possibility that the South opened the fighting on Ongjin, with an eye to seizing Haeju, cannot be discounted, but there is no evidence that it intended a general invasion.

The question pregnant with ideological dynamite, 'Who started the Korean war?', is surely the wrong question. No Americans care any more that the South fired first on Fort Sumter in their Civil War; they do still care about slavery and secession. No one asks who started the Vietnam war. Like Vietnam, Korea was a civil and revolutionary war.

### From Seoul to Pusan to Inchon: the War for Containment

Word of fighting in Korea arrived in Washington on Saturday night, 24 June. In succeeding days Dean Acheson dominated the decision-making that soon committed American air and ground forces to the fight. Acheson (along with Dean Rusk) made the decision to take the Korean question to the UN before he had notified President Truman of the fighting;

Acheson greets Truman on Sunday, 25 June, after the President's return from Missouri, while Secretary of Defense Louis Johnson keeps his eye on the Secretary of State.

Acheson told Truman that there was no need to have him back in Washington until the next day. At meetings on the evening of 25 June Acheson argued for increased military aid to the South, American air cover for evacuation and the interposition of the American 7th Fleet between Taiwan and the mainland; on the afternoon of 26 June Acheson laboured alone on the fundamental decisions committing American air and naval power to the Korean war. Thus the decision to intervene was Acheson's, supported by the President but taken without United Nations, Pentagon or Congressional approval.

The military representatives offered the only opposition to American intervention. General Omar Bradley supported Acheson's containment policy at the first meeting, remarking, 'We must draw the line somewhere.' But he questioned the 'advisability' of introducing American

An American Douglas C–54 transport on fire at Kimpo airport, 28 June 1950, after being hit by North Korean fighters.

ground troops in large numbers, as did Frank Pace and Louis Johnson. At the second meeting on 26 June Generals Bradley and Collins again expressed the view that committing ground troops would strain American combat-troop limits unless a general mobilization were undertaken.

The United Nations was used to ratify American decisions. As an official Joint Chiefs of Staff study put it, 'Having resolved upon armed intervention for itself, the US government the next day sought the approval and the assistance of the United Nations,' an accurate judgement.

UNCOK's 26 June report blamed the fighting entirely on the North and provided the slender information upon which the United Nations committed itself to the fighting. UNCOK's report said:

> Commission's present view on basis evidence is, first, that judging from actual progress of operations northern regime is carrying out well-planned, concerted and full-scale invasion of South Korea, second, that South Korean forces were deployed on wholly defensive basis in all sectors of the parallel, and third, that

Women at Taegu army depot watching as their menfolk go off for training in the South Korean Army, summer 1950.

they were taken completely by surprise as they had no reason to believe from intelligence sources that invasion was imminent.

UNCOK's report was drafted on the morning of 26 June, then finalized in Japan on 29 June; it was based exclusively on American and South Korean sources and on its observers' report, on which some preliminary work had been done on 24 June, before the hostilities commenced. Even on 25 June the two military observers reported that they were 'having trouble getting information'; on 27 June all UNCOK members were evacuated to Japan on American military transport. Eight members arrived back in Pusan from Tokyo on 30 June. This means, of course, that UNCOK members woke up in Seoul on Sunday morning to a war, wrote a report based on the limited observations of two people and whatever the Koreans and Americans chose to tell them, and then were in the care of the American military for the next three days. They left all their archives behind in Seoul, making it impossible to verify the information that UNCOK had at its disposal.

United Nations backing was crucial to the war of opinion, which the USA was thereby enabled to win on a world scale, making its official view of what happened definitive and lasting. Acheson later said that UNCOK's report was of 'invaluable assistance' in confirming that

# Where UN forces came from

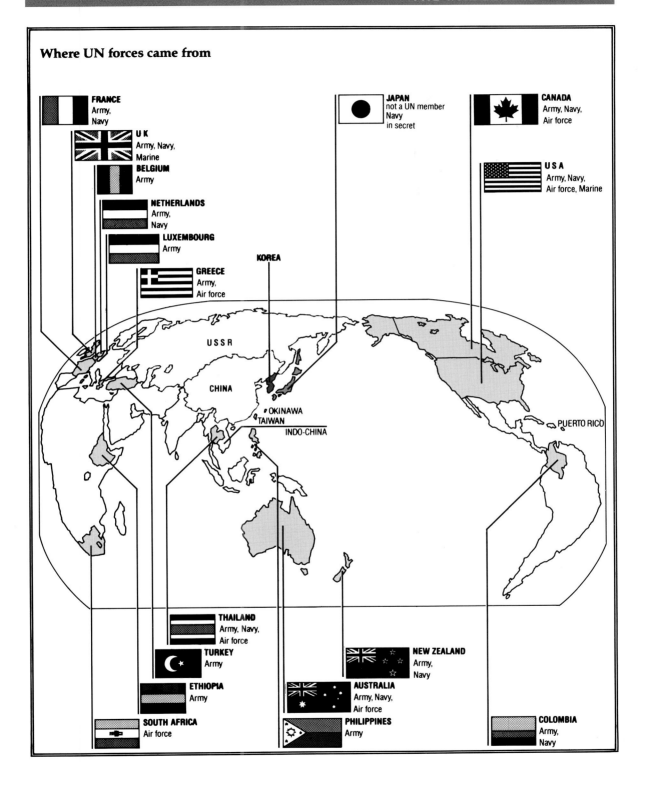

**FRANCE**
Army,
Navy

**UK**
Army, Navy,
Marine

**BELGIUM**
Army

**NETHERLANDS**
Army,
Navy

**LUXEMBOURG**
Army

**GREECE**
Army,
Air force

**JAPAN**
not a UN member
Navy
in secret

**CANADA**
Army, Navy,
Air force

**USA**
Army, Navy,
Air force, Marine

KOREA

USSR

CHINA

OKINAWA
TAIWAN
INDO-CHINA

PUERTO RICO

**THAILAND**
Army, Navy,
Air force

**TURKEY**
Army

**ETHIOPIA**
Army

**SOUTH AFRICA**
Air force

**NEW ZEALAND**
Army,
Navy

**AUSTRALIA**
Army, Navy,
Air force

**PHILIPPINES**
Army

**COLOMBIA**
Army,
Navy

South Korea was the 'unprepared victim [of] deliberate assault'. Member states were slow to commit forces to the battle, however. Ultimately the British made more of a stand than anyone else; by the spring of 1951 the totals showed about 12,000 British soldiers, 8,500 Canadians, 5,000 Turks, 5,000 Filipinos and other contingents below 1,000. The USA paid most of the bill for the allied troops.

Among the obscure and anomalous events still resistant to explanation and logic in connection with the Korean decision not the least is the USSR's absence from the Security Council in June – which invalidated its much used veto mechanism. Soviet envoy Jacob Malik was boycotting the Security Council, ostensibly because the UN had refused to admit China. (The boycott had begun in January 1950.) He was planning to return to Moscow for consultations on 6 July.

There is now evidence that the Soviet delegation was explicitly ordered to stay away from the UN when the war began. Why? Logic would suggest one of two possibilities. First, Stalin wanted to suck the United States into a war in peripheral Korea, hoping ultimately to blood the Chinese against American soldiers; UN backing would greatly boost a policy of intervention. Second, Stalin may have hoped that cloaking American intervention in the UN flag would destroy this body or at least would reveal it to be an American tool.

When the war began the Soviet information apparatus was silent for three days except to repeat some of Pyongyang's statements verbatim and without comment. But from day one the USSR made clear its determination to stay clear of the fighting. In the early morning hours of 26 June Russian ships which had sailed from the Soviet-controlled port of Dairen in China, just opposite Korea, were ordered 'to return to their own defence zone immediately'. Soviet naval vessels also stayed clear of the war zone, and from 25 June onwards their submarines never interfered with American shipping. The USSR also pulled back its advisers with the KPA. Daily field-situation reports were generally negative about any direct participation by Soviet officers in the war, though they occasionally cited evidence of Soviet advisers remaining in the North with air and naval units.

There is no evidence of an upturn in Soviet military shipments to North Korea after 25 June; instead, if anything, a decrease was registered. By and large the only equipment the Americans captured that could clearly have been new equipment stockpiled for an invasion was trucks with low mileage on their odometers. In September 1950 MacArthur had 'physical proof' of only ten military items delivered to the North Koreans in 1949 and 1950 – some machine-guns, grenades, radio receivers and the like. By early September 1950 intelligence sources told *The New York Times* that they had 'no knowledge that the North Korean invaders actually received new supplies from the Soviet Union since the war began'. We are thus left to reconcile the American assumption that Stalin started the war with the unambiguous evidence that he distanced Soviet prestige and armed might from the conflict.

**South Korean students rally to the North Koreans, Seoul, summer 1950.** ▷

KPA Soldiers and people
dancing in Seoul (summer
1950).

KPA forces
arrive in
Seoul.

△

A celebration of the fifth
anniversary of the
Liberation, 15 August
1950, with an American
POW present.

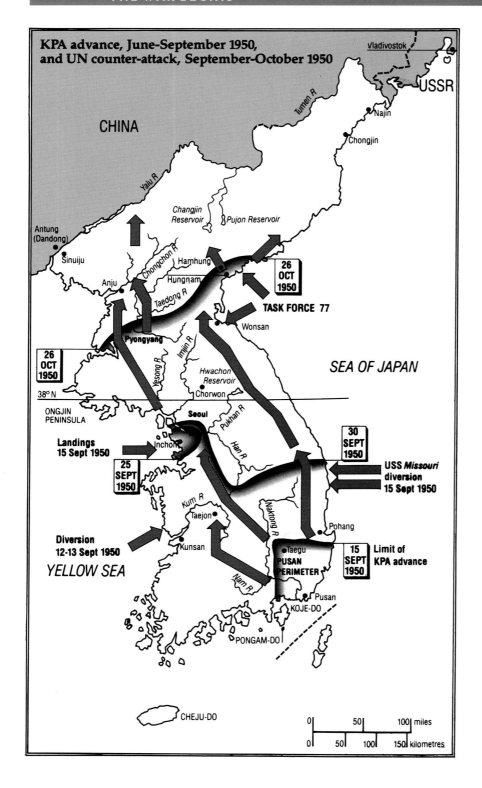

KPA advance, June–September 1950,
and UN counter-attack, September–October 1950

CHINA

USSR

Vladivostok

Najin

Chongjin

Yalu R.

Tumen R.

Antung
(Dandong)

Sinuiju

Anju

Chongchon R.

Changjin
Reservoir

Pujon Reservoir

Hamhung

Hungnam

**26
OCT
1950**

**TASK FORCE 77**

Taedong R.

**Pyongyang**

Wonsan

**SEA OF JAPAN**

**26
OCT
1950**

Yesong R.

Imjin R.

Hwachon
Reservoir

Chorwon

38° N

ONGJIN
PENINSULA

**Seoul**

Pukhan R.

**30
SEPT
1950**

Landings
15 Sept 1950

Inchon

Han R.

**25
SEPT
1950**

USS *Missouri*
diversion
15 Sept 1950

Kum R.

Naktong R.

Taejon

Pohang

Diversion
12-13 Sept 1950

Kunsan

Taegu

**15
SEPT
1950**

Limit of
KPA advance

**YELLOW SEA**

**PUSAN
PERIMETER**

Nam R.

Pusan

KOJE-DO

PONGAM-DO

CHEJU-DO

| 0 | | 50 | | 100 | miles |
|---|---|---|---|---|---|
| 0 | 50 | 100 | | 150 | kilometres |

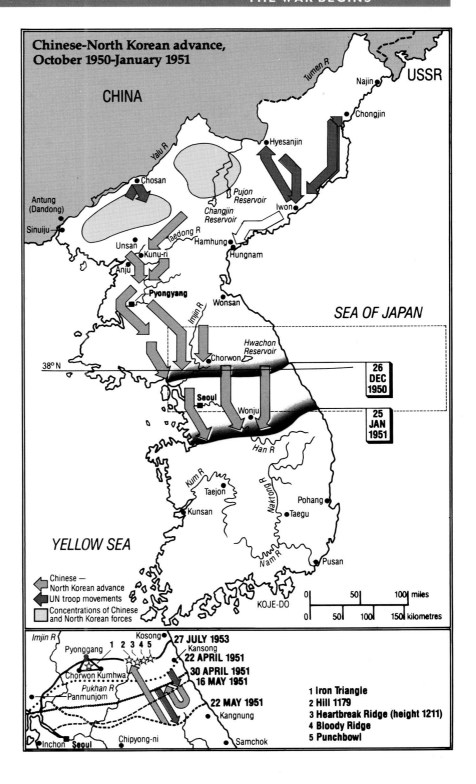

**Chinese-North Korean advance,
October 1950-January 1951**

CHINA

USSR

Tumen R

Najin

Chongjin

Hyesanjin

Yalu R

Chosan

Pujon
Reservoir

Antung
(Dandong)

Changjin
Reservoir

Iwon

Sinuiju

Taedong R

Hamhung

Unsan

Kunu-ri

Hungnam

Anju

**Pyongyang**

Wonsan

SEA OF JAPAN

Imjin R

Hwachon
Reservoir

Chorwon

38° N

**26
DEC
1950**

**Seoul**

Wonju

**25
JAN
1951**

Han R

Kum R

Taejon

Naktong R

Pohang

Kunsan

Taegu

YELLOW SEA

Nam R

Pusan

Chinese —
North Korean advance

UN troop movements

Concentrations of Chinese
and North Korean forces

KOJE-DO

0      50      100 miles

0    50    100    150 kilometres

Imjin R

Kosong

**27 JULY 1953**

Pyonggang    1  2  3  4  5

Kansong

**22 APRIL 1951**

Chorwon Kumhwa

**30 APRIL 1951**
**16 MAY 1951**

Pukhan R
Panmunjom

**22 MAY 1951**

Kangnung

**1 Iron Triangle**
**2 Hill 1179**
**3 Heartbreak Ridge (height 1211)**
**4 Bloody Ridge**
**5 Punchbowl**

Inchon   **Seoul**

Chipyong-ni

Samchok

The Chinese response was quicker than that of the USSR and less non-committal. The official *People's Daily* published its first editorial on 27 June, a day before the first Moscow editorial, and it said much more. The Chinese lambasted the Rhee regime as an American puppet, cited its many provocations of the North and criticized American policy, following the North Korean line. As the war and American involvement developed, the Chinese assumed some measure of responsibility for North Korea's fate that predated their actual intervention by months and went quite beyond the Soviet position.

The first of August was Armed Forces Day in China, and Chinese authorities used the occasion to criticize American imperialism, calling the North Korean battle 'completely just' and referring to the North as 'our good neighbour'. In mid-August the Americans picked up growing evidence of Chinese backing for the North. Intelligence sources later claimed that the Chinese had pledged to furnish 250,000 soldiers for Korea in a high-level Beijing meeting on 14 August, and by the end of the month a huge Sino-Korean army was poised on the Chinese border with Korea. On 21 July Zhou Enlai assured Indian Ambassador Panikkar that the Chinese had every intention of staying out of the Korean hostilities, but by late August he had inaugurated the steady drumbeat of warnings that, in retrospect, clearly foreshadowed the Chinese entry into the war.

**South Korean soldiers tending to wounded woman with child, *c.* August 1950.**

### The Drive on Pusan

In the summer months of 1950 the North Korean Army pushed southwards with extraordinary success and, until the US First Marine Division stiffened the defence, with one humiliating defeat of American forces after another. An Army that had bested Germany and Japan found its back pressed to the wall by what seemed to be a hastily assembled peasant military said to be doing the bidding of a foreign imperial power.

After the capture of Seoul, the North Korean Army waited about a week to make its next big push, which resulted in the capture of Taejon in what most analysts thought to be one of the North's finest battles. In early July American daily situation reports said that the KPA infantry was 'first-class', its armour and service 'unsurpassed in World War II'. Americans were especially impressed with the 6th Division (formed entirely of 'CCF Koreans' and led by Pang Ho-san), which participated in the initial fighting on Ongjin, swept southwards along the coast through the Chollas, then by the end of July abruptly turned east, occupying Chinju by 1 August and thereby directly menacing Pusan. But the initial delay south of Seoul, probably occasioned by the necessity to bring up artillery and other supplies from the rear, gave MacArthur the time necessary to organize a defence.

By the beginning of August American and South Korean forces outnumbered the North's along the front 92,000 to 70,000 (47,000 were Americans), but in spite of this the retreat continued. MacArthur hid

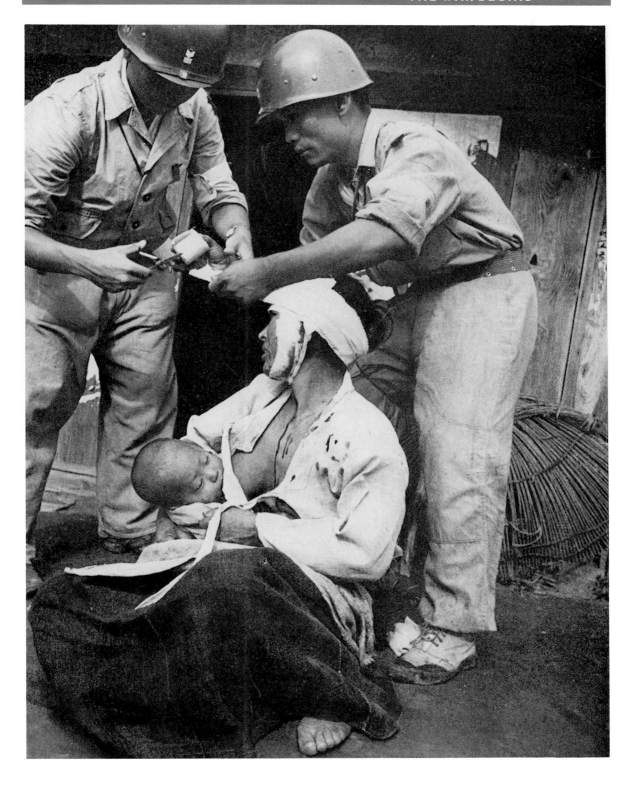

KPA soldiers roll into Taejon.

this from other American officials, claiming that his forces were outnumbered two or three to one. In the first week of August, however, the First Marine Division went into action and finally halted the North's advance. The front did not change much from that point until the end of August.

The Pusan perimeter had its northern anchor on the coast around Pohang, its southern anchor in the Chinju–Masan region and its centre just above the major city of Taegu. The latter became a symbol of the American determination to stanch the KPA's advance; for Koreans it was even more important as a major stronghold of the Southern left. But it was Pohang in the North that was probably the key to stopping the KPA from occupying Pusan and throwing the Americans into the sea. Appleman wrote that the 'major tactical mistake' of the North Koreans was not to press their advantage on the eastern coastal road. The North's 5th Division worried too much about covering its flanks instead of moving quickly on Pohang and thence combining with the 6th Division to threaten Pusan.

Throughout the summer of 1950 Northern troops were aided by guerrillas, most of them local but some from the North. From 25 June to 31 August an average of 100 guerrilla casualties per day were recorded, with total losses of 67,228 killed, 23,837 captured and 44,154 surrendered. That is more than double the total number of Americans killed in action during the entire war. During the weeks of the struggle on the Pusan perimeter large units had to be diverted to secure rear areas infested with guerrillas.

Americans first felt the combination of frontal assault and guerrilla warfare in the battle for Taejon. Local peasants, including women and children, would come running along the hillsides near the battle lines as if they were refugees. 'At a given signal, the "refugees" snatched rifles, machine-guns and hand grenades from their bundles and brought down withering fire on the troops below.' The retreat from Taejon ran into well-

A cartoon of MacArthur from the Soviet satirical magazine *Krokodil*, early August 1950. In another context MacArthur remarked that he had always been able 'to take care of the enemy in my front – but have never been able to protect myself from shafts from the rear'.

organized roadblocks and ambushes, often placed by local residents. Americans thought anyone in 'white pyjamas' (thus they described the Korean native dress) might potentially be an enemy. From this point onwards American forces began burning villages suspected of harbouring guerrillas, and in some cases they were burned merely to deny hiding places to the guerrillas.

We have argued that the war originated in the collapse of Japan's colonial empire and that it was a civil war. In the midst of the massive push towards Pusan thousands of Korean cadres, from North and South, set about restoring the people's committees disbanded in 1945–6 and pushing through land redistribution on a revolutionary basis. Through it all they beat the drum of Korean unification and independence. The North Korean occupation of the South is thus an essential ingredient in determining this war's origins and what manner of war it was.

**Women's meeting, Seoul, summer 1950.**

Kim Il Sung called for the restoration of the people's committees in his first radio address after the war broke out, and American intelligence recognized the crucial importance to the North Koreans of the revival of this political form, 'dissolved long ago by US Army military government'. Propagandists referred to this point over and over again and counterposed the committee form with the reimposition of what they called the 'ruling organs of Japanese imperialism'. In other words, from their point of view

Interrogation of a woman
Korean People's Army
soldier, captured in late
July 1950.

the goal was to restore people's committees, which pre-dated the reimposition of the colonial state.

The Seoul people's committee formed quickly, led mostly by
Southerners. By early July the administration had confiscated all Japanese
property and that of the ROK government, its officials and 'monopoly
capitalists'. The KPA distributed stored rice stocks to the poor and left the
administration of justice in the hands of local people, many of whom had
just been released from prison. In the early days prisoners released from
Rhee's jails carried out a reign of terror against their former antagonists,
mostly those in the police and youth groups.

About sixty members of the ROK National Assembly
remained in Seoul, and towards the end of July forty-eight of them held a
meeting expressing their allegiance to the North. Even one American did
the bidding of the regime, whether voluntarily or not. 'Seoul City Sue', the

Tokyo Rose of the Korean war, broadcast appeals to American soldiers over Seoul radio in an unmistakably native accent. She was Anne Wallace Suhr, a former Methodist missionary married to a Korean leftist.

The occupation ended amid the crisis of the Inchon landing and the renewed vicious battle for Seoul. Discipline broke down, and many killings occurred. Buildings were also burned, apparently by vagrants and children who were urged on by the KPA.

Throughout the rest of South Korea local people's committees re-emerged but not in the spontaneous fashion of 1945. The North Koreans exercised sharp procedural controls to ensure that committee membership would conform to North Korean practice and discipline. The restoration of the committees was relatively easy compared with the attempt to carry through revolutionary land reform in the midst of a war. But a confrontation with Korea's landed class, which had previously succeeded in blocking the reformist redistribution forced on the ROK by the Americans, was taken to be the essence of the anti-feudal, anti-colonial character of the Korean revolution. The redistribution ensued in every province outside the Pusan perimeter; although it was hasty and done in wartime conditions, it cleared away class structures and power that later made possible Rhee's land-redistribution programme – because the Americans would not fight merely to restore land to this class that had ruled Korea for centuries.

**Guerrillas captured near Chonsu in South Korea, 12 July 1950.**

The North Koreans fought a war on all fronts: a conventional war, a guerrilla war and a political war over the people's committees and land reform. In other words, in some sense this was a people's war, and, like the subsequent war in Vietnam, it called forth an appalling American response. *Collier's* magazine began an article by saying, 'Our Red foe scorns all rules of civilized warfare, hid[ing] behind women's skirts', then quoted the following colloquy between American soldiers:

The young pilot drained his cup of coffee and said, 'Hell's fire, you can't shoot people when they stand there waving at you.' 'Shoot 'em,' he was told firmly. 'They're troops.' 'But, hell, they've all got on those white pajama things and they're straggling down the road' . . . 'See any women or children?' 'Women? I wouldn't know. The women wear pants, too, don't they? But no kids, no, sir.' 'They're troops. Shoot 'em.'

Reginald Thompson, a sensitive British war correspondent, wrote in *Cry Korea*, 'There were few who dared to write the truth of things as they saw them.' Journalists found the campaign for the South 'strangely disturbing', very different from World War II in its guerrilla and popular aspects. Thompson witnessed an American Marine kill an elderly civilian as if in a fit of absent-mindedness, showing no sign of remorse, and remarked that GIs 'never spoke of the enemy as though they were people, but as one might speak of apes'. Even among correspondents 'every man's dearest wish was to kill a Korean. "Today . . . I'll get me a gook."' Americans called Koreans 'gooks', he thought, because 'otherwise these essentially kind and generous Americans would not have been able to kill them indiscriminately or smash up their homes and poor belongings'.

Charles Grutzner, who reported the war for *The New York Times*, said that in the early stages 'fear of infiltrators led to the slaughter of hundreds of South Korean civilians, women as well as men, by some US troops and police of the Republic.' He quoted a high-ranking US officer who told him of an American regiment that panicked in July and shot 'many civilians'. Keyes Beech, another American correspondent, wrote, 'It is not the time to be a Korean, for the Yankees are shooting them all . . . nervous American troops are ready to fire at any Korean.'

Reginald Thompson found himself sickened by the carnage of the American air war, machined military might used against 'an almost unarmed enemy, unable to challenge the aircraft in the skies'. In September 1950 'handfuls of peasants defied the immense weight of modern arms with a few rifles and carbines and a hopeless courage . . . and brought down upon themselves and all the inhabitants the appalling horror of jellied petrol bombs.' Every enemy shot, he said, 'released a deluge of destruction. Every village and township in the path of war was blotted out.' In such warfare 'the slayer needs merely touch a button, and death is on the wing, blindly blotting out the remote, the unknown people, holocausts of death, veritable mass productions of death, spreading an abysmal desolation over whole communities.'

Perhaps the most daunting story is that from the first days of the war the Americans contemplated the use of atomic weapons in this 'limited' war. On 9 July – a mere two weeks into the war, it is worth remembering – MacArthur sent Ridgway a 'hot message' that prompted the Joint Chiefs of Staff 'to consider whether or not A-bombs should be made available to MacArthur'.

General Bolté, Chief of Operations, was asked to talk to

Cartoon from the North Korean satirical magazine *Hwalsal* ('Arrow'):

'Where are the Partisans?'

'Over there.'

The American comic *Two-fisted Tales* portrays the 'gook' issue – behind the lines.

MacArthur about using atomic bombs 'in direct support [of] ground combat'; some ten to twenty bombs could be spared without 'unduly' jeopardizing the general war plan. Bolté got from MacArthur one of the earliest suggestions for the tactical use of atomic weapons and an indication of MacArthur's extraordinary ambitions for the war, which included occupying the North and handling potential Chinese – or Soviet – intervention as follows: 'I would cut them off in North Korea. In Korea I visualize a cul-de-sac. The only passages leading from Manchuria and Vladivostok have many tunnels and bridges. I see here a unique use for the atomic bomb – to strike a blocking blow – which would require a six-months repair job. Sweeten up my B–29 force . . .' At this point in the war, however, the Joint Chiefs of Staff rejected use of the bomb.

All sides in the war were guilty of atrocities. KPA forces executed several hundreds of American prisoners of war, albeit usually in the traditional battlefield 'humane' manner: one bullet behind the ear. Treatment of ROK prisoners of war was said to be considerably worse, but there is little evidence of this. There were a number of brutal atrocities against civilians, especially as the occupation of the South ended.

The United Nations archive contains well-documented accounts, verified by witnesses and relatives, of several mass murders of Southerners by the Northern occupants, including a particularly ghastly one at Chonju. For what it is worth, captured North Korean documents continued to show that high-level officials warned against executing people. Several orders to stop any further executions were picked up on the battlefield; handwritten minutes of a party meeting, apparently at a high level, said, 'Do not execute the reactionaries for [their] wanton vengeance. Let legal authorities carry out the purge plan.'

It has been alleged that the North Koreans perpetrated one of the greatest mass killings of the war in Taejon, where between 5,000 and 7,000 people were slaughtered and placed in mass graves. Some Americans were included; in one incident six survivors, including two Americans, were found alive, feigning death under the light soil thrown on top of them. Mass burial graves were reputedly also found at many points in South Cholla, and Appleman writes that the North Koreans 'ran amok' in Wonju on 2 October, killing between 1,000 and 2,000 civilians.

What actually happened in the Taejon atrocity is not at all clear, however. In early August Alan Winnington published an article in the London *Daily Worker* entitled 'US Belsen in Korea', alleging that the South Korean police, under the supervision of American advisers, had butchered 7,000 people in the village of Yangwol, near Taejon, during the period 2–6 July. He visited the area and found twenty eyewitnesses who said that on 2 July truckloads of police arrived and made local people dig six pits, each 200 yards long. Two days later political prisoners were trucked in and executed, by bullets to the head and decapitation by the sword, and layered on top of each other in the pits 'like sardines'. The massacres continued for three days. The witnesses said that US officers in two jeeps observed the killings.

**Two American soldiers pose with a KPA prisoner, 5 August 1950.**

North Korean sources said 4,000 had been killed (changing the total some months later to 7,000), comprising mostly imprisoned guerrillas from Cheju Island and the Taebaek-san area and those detained after the Yosu–Sunchon incident. They located the site differently, placing the events at Chango village in Sanae township, Taedok county.

**South Korean political prisoner at Pusan, summer 1950.**

The American Embassy in London called the Winnington story an 'atrocity fabrication', however, and denied its contents. British officials in Tokyo said, 'There may be an element of truth in this report.'

There is undeniable evidence of South Korean massacres on a lesser scale. A *New York Times* reporter found an ROK policeman with forty civilians in his retinue, alleged guerrillas, observing him as he 'crashed the butt of his rifle on the back of one after another'. 'We bang-bang in the woods,' the policeman said happily, meaning that the prisoners would be 'taken into the groves and executed after their backs had been broken.' An Australian witnessed a similar incident in Kongju, where twenty civilian prisoners were kneeling and being beaten by guards 'on [the] least movement'. On inquiry the guards said, 'Guerrillas, bang-bang.' A *Manchester Guardian* correspondent saw a truckload of sixty prisoners taken to the Kum river on 12 July and executed by ROK authorities. 'Tiger' Kim had fifty North Korean prisoners of war beheaded in August; when the Red Cross made representations to KMAG about it, KMAG officers said they 'would not like to see it get in the hands of correspondents'.

James Cameron of London's *Picture Post* wrote about what he termed 'South Korean concentration camps' in Pusan in the late summer of 1950:

> I had seen Belsen, but this was worse. This terrible mob of men –
> convicted of nothing, un-tried, South Koreans in South Korea,
> suspected of being 'unreliable'. There were hundreds of them;
> they were skeletal, puppets of string, faces translucent grey,
> manacled to each other with chains, cringing in the classic Orien-
> tal attitude of subjection, the squatting foetal position, in piles of
> garbage . . . Around this medievally gruesome market-place
> were gathered a few knots of American soldiers photographing
> the scene with casual industry . . . I took my indignation to the
> [UN] Commission, who said very civilly: 'Most disturbing, yes;
> but remember these are Asian people, with different standards of
> behaviour . . . all very difficult.' It was supine and indefensible
> compromise. I boiled, and I do not boil easily. We recorded the
> situation meticulously, in words and photographs. Within the
> year it nearly cost me my job, and my magazine its existence.

*Picture Post* never published Cameron's story, causing a 'mini-mutiny' on the magazine; shortly thereafter *Picture Post* 'withered away, as it deserved'.

At the end of August Northern forces launched their last major offensive, making in the next two weeks 'startling gains' that severely strained the American–Korean lines. On 28 August Pang Ho-san ordered his troops to take Masan and Pusan in the next few days; three battalions succeeded in crossing the Naktong river in the central sector; Pohang and Chinju were taken; and the perimeter was 'near the breaking point', with Northern forces again pressing on Kyongju, Masan and Taegu. General Walker moved Eighth Army headquarters from Taegu to Pusan; other high officials were evacuated from Taegu; and prominent Koreans began leaving Pusan for Cheju or Tsushima Island. On 9 September Kim Il Sung said the war had reached an 'extremely harsh, decisive stage', with the enemy being pressed on three fronts; General Walker two days later reported that the front-line situation was the most dangerous since the perimeter was established. Appleman wrote that by mid-September, 'after two weeks of the heaviest fighting of the war, [American forces] had just barely turned back the great North Korean offensive.' By 15 September American battle casualties were over 19,000, with 4,280 dead.

North Korea had raised the number of its forces along the front to 98,000, but more than one-third of them were new, raw recruits. Guerrillas, including many women, were quite active in the fighting in both the Pohang and the Masan area, however. Still, the North Koreans were by then badly outnumbered. MacArthur had succeeded in committing most of the battle-ready divisions in the American Army to the Korean fighting; by 8 September he had been sent all available trained Army units except for the 82nd Airborne Division. By the time of the Inchon landing some 83,000 American soldiers and another 57,000 Korean and British faced the North Koreans at the front.

**A multinational force holds the line near the Naktong river, September 1950: an Englishman, an Australian, an American and two South Koreans.**

# THE WAR FOR THE NORTH

In mid-September 1950 MacArthur masterminded his last hurrah, a tactically brilliant amphibious landing at Inchon that brought American armed forces back to Seoul nearly five years to the day after they had first set foot on Korean soil. Inchon harbour has treacherous tides that can easily ground a flotilla of ships if the wrong time is chosen, but the American passage through the shifting bays and flats was technically flawless. American marines landed almost unopposed but then slogged through a deadly gauntlet before Seoul finally fell at the end of September.

Admiral Arthur Dewey Struble, the Navy's crack amphibious expert who had led the landing operations at Leyte in the Philippines and who directed the naval operations off Omaha Beach during the Normandy invasion, commanded an enormous fleet of 261 ships in the Inchon operations, depositing the Marines with hardly a loss. Against this the North Koreans could do nothing. They were not surprised by the invasion, as the American mythology has it, but could not resist it, and so began what their historians call euphemistically the 'temporary strategic retreat'.

The Inchon landing allowed the UN forces to break out of the Pusan perimeter within days. The first Korean war ended on 30 September as ROK Army units crossed into the North, pressing a rollback against rapidly withdrawing Northern forces. The war for the South left 111,000 South Koreans killed, 106,000 wounded and 57,000 missing; 314,000 homes had been destroyed, 244,000 damaged. American casualties totalled nearly 5,000 dead, 13,659 wounded and 3,877 missing in action. North Korean casualty figures are not known. Now a new war began: an advance into the maw of a combined army of Chinese and Koreans waiting in the mountain fastness of the Sino-Korean border.

The North Korean thrust southwards had seemed immediately to stimulate American thinking of a thrust northwards. In late June Dulles is reported as saying, 'in a desultory way', that the Korean incident might be used to go beyond the parallel. In mid-July John Allison prepared a top-secret memo for Rusk, arguing that the parallel was quite different from the boundaries in Central Europe. It had no *de jure* significance, after all. The record, he said, showed 'that this line was agreed upon only for the surrender of Japanese troops and that the US had made no commitments with regard to the continuing validity of the line for any other purpose'. The right, of course, also wanted rollback, but so did the liberals in the State

**Commonwealth soldiers sport with pictures of Kim and Stalin as they advance into the North, October 1950.**

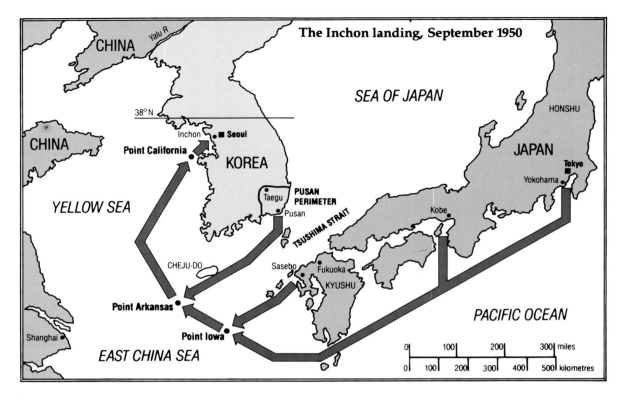

The Inchon landing, September 1950

Department. MacArthur was correct in telling Senators in 1951 that the crossing of the parallel 'had the most complete and absolute approval of every section of the American government', if we grant him the licence of mild exaggeration.

The momentum of the Inchon landing carried UN forces across the parallel and deep into North Korean territory; it was also thought to have completely destroyed the North Korean Army. In early October Southern units swept up the east coast with next to no resistance. They were 25 miles above the parallel within two days, had four divisions in the North within a week and captured the eastern port city of Wonsan on 10 October. Thereafter they kept on rolling towards the Yalu, with the North Korean Army withdrawing ahead of them – an odd and heady new reality for an army that, a few weeks earlier, had been judged continuously to 'break' under North Korean pressure. After a week of marching in the North, a South Korean major kept repeating that he could not understand why the North had been 'giving up beautiful natural defences', causing a reporter to comment that the North Koreans 'have not been fighting' and that the quality of their soldiers had clearly been overrated.

American forces faced stiffer opposition on the western side, but by mid-October MacArthur's headquarters announced 'spectacular gains'; the communist capital was seized. *The New York Times* wrote that the final phase of the war was at hand and ran a banner headline saying, 'UN

*Above and overleaf:*
**American soldiers go over a wall during the Inchon landing, which was mostly unopposed.**

troops race unopposed toward the Manchurian border'. Some commentators proclaimed a 'smashing North Korean defeat', and cigars were lit all over Tokyo and Washington.

In many ways, however, the Inchon victory was pyrrhic. MacArthur and his advisers, fighting a guerrilla war as a conventional war, were drawn into a morass. Reginald Thompson wrote, 'The North Korean Army had disappeared like a wraith into the hills . . . The trap had closed, and it was empty.' A discerning London *Times* account carried a sentence that would seem incomprehensible in the light of received wisdom on the post-Inchon fighting: 'The aggressiveness of the rearguard suggests that there is a future Korean Mao Tse-tung in Kanggye.' It went on that a 'dangerous complacency' had overtaken American officers: 'The enemy's forces were declared to have been destroyed when elements of twelve divisions were identified . . . the intrinsic strength and pliability of communist armies were forgotten . . . Fears that large numbers of communists and their followers withdrawing into the northern hills would wage a partisan war had been realized.' Among American reporters only the Asia hand Walter Sullivan understood that many Northern officers had fought with the Chinese and were now following 'Chinese communist' strategies of withdrawal and retreat, preparations for these having been made over the previous three months.

Inchon after 'liberation'. South Korean Marines and civilian inhabitants.

Bert Hardy, who took this photograph, captioned it 'The morning of Inchon's "liberation". As the picture[s] show, no one could feel safe.'

US troops with captured guerrillas, Anyang, 22 September 1950, just after the Inchon landing and the break-out from the Pusan Perimeter.

Korean People's Army soldiers captured at Wolmi Island and forced to undress completely, 20 September 1950.

**An old man hit by napalm during the fighting for Inchon and Seoul.**

A captured North Korean officer's notebook said that after the Inchon landing, 'The main force of the enemy still remained intact, not having been fully damaged. When they were not fully aware of the power of our forces, they pushed their infantry far forward . . . to the Yalu river. This indicates that they underestimated us. All these conditions were favourable to lure them near us . . .

Of course, Inchon was still a bad defeat for the North. Entire units in the 3rd Division panicked and collapsed, according to Appleman, and the 8th Division lost 4,000 casualties; the 12th was completely destroyed after fighting 'stubborn delaying actions'. Huge quantities of equipment were lost; the morale of troops and civilians was badly affected. The retreat made the best of a bad deal that North Korea could do little about, an enormous amphibious invasion.

'Meanwhile, a crowd had gathered, and a group of prisoners, already stripped naked, were forced to a halt. In the front were two young women who had been permitted to retain long pantaloons which they held with difficulty to hide their breasts. Two or three reporters stayed to investigate, and later it was discovered that the women were nurses, and that some of their number had been shot "trying to escape" when the troops burst in on them' (Reginald Thompson, *Cry Korea*, p. 70). It is not certain that this is the scene to which Thompson refers, but the place and time are right. The caption says the women had been firing guns but claimed to be nurses.

American soldiers in the fighting for Seoul, late September 1950.

KPA Colonel Li Hak Ku after surrender, 21 September 1950. Li was the highest-ranking KPA officer captured by the UN and was considered a prize catch. Later he emerged as the leader of the POW revolts on Koje, and it was thought that he surrendered deliberately at this point, when large numbers of KPA were being captured, in order to provide political leadership for the POWs.

Repairing a bridge in South Korea during the communist occupation.

Seoul's Capitol building after its partial burning by departing North Koreans. The former centre of the Japanese colonial government, the building was constructed to represent the first character of the word 'Nippon'.

Digging trenches in front of Seoul railway station during the period when it was held by the communists, probably September 1950.

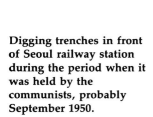

### The South Occupies the North

Just as the North imposed its politics on the South, so the reverse happened. The effective politics of the Southern occupation consisted mostly of the National Police and the rightist youths who trundled along with it. Cho Pyong-ok was now Home Minister, and on 10 October he announced that the National Police controlled nine towns north of the parallel, with a special force of 30,000 being recruited for occupation duty.

State Department officials had sought some mechanism for supervision of the political aspects of the rollback, 'to ensure that a "bloodbath" would not result. In other words . . . the Korean forces should be kept under control.' Shortly the Embassy's Everett Drumwright said the Department's plans were 'already outmoded by events', with some 2,000 National Police across the parallel; he suggested that perhaps more local responsibility would result if police who originally came from the North could be used. By 20 October, if not earlier, rightist youth corps were conducting 'political indoctrination' in the North.

The Pyongyang occupation was a disgrace. American Civil Affairs officers were 'pathetically few' and barely experienced.

> The recruitment of a provisional city council for Pyongyang would have been farcical, if the implications were not so obviously tragic. It was rather like watching an Army sergeant selecting men for fatigue duty. As a result, weeks after the fall of the city there were no public utilities, law and order was evident only on the main streets during the hours of daylight, and the food shortage due to indifferent transport and distribution had assumed serious proportions.

107

*Top*: A wounded KPA prisoner (dabbing his wound with a cloth) in a US jeep at the thirty-eighth parallel, 18 October 1950.

△
A GI munches a cookie as he observes a dead Korean soldier, Sariwon, North Korea, 18 October 1950.

△
Bob Hope and Marilyn Maxwell with Mrs Rhee and Syngman Rhee, 23 October 1950.

American soldiers fight in ▷ a Pyongyang railway yard, October 1950.

Kim Il Sung, *centre*, in Pyongyang, apparently leaving a ceremony (date unknown).

American soldiers take coffee in front of camouflaged Capitol building, Pyongyang, 21 October 1950.

This agency photograph was captioned: 'It's Round-up Time in Korea.' Mounted South Korean soldiers 'ride herd' on a prisoner as he is marched through a Pyongyang street to a prisoner-collection point in the North Korean capital. A bicycling North Korean, wearing an armband identifying him as an anti-communist, joins the parade.

By the end of October the British had clear evidence that the ROK, as a matter of official policy, sought to 'hunt out and destroy communists and collaborators'; this information came from both their own people and experienced British correspondents like Louis Heren of the London *Times*; the facts confirmed 'what is now becoming pretty notorious, namely that the restored civil administration in Korea bids fair to become an international scandal of a major kind'. The Foreign Office urged that immediate representations be made in Washington, given that the ROK was acting under the name of the UN and because this was 'a war for men's minds' in which the political counted almost as much as the military. Ambassador Franks brought the matter up with Dean Rusk on 30 October, getting this response: 'Rusk agrees that there have regrettably been many cases of atrocities' by the ROK authorities. Rusk promised to have American military officers seek to control the situation.

### The Chinese Entry into the War

The general conclusion of all American intelligence agencies was that China would not come into the war, although on 20 September the CIA envisaged the possibility that Chinese 'volunteers' might enter the fighting, and a month later it noted 'a number of reports' that Manchurian units would be sent to Korea. However, it said, 'The odds are that communist China, like the USSR, will not openly intervene in North Korea.' On 1 November the new head of the CIA, Bedell Smith, wrote accurately that the Chinese 'probably genuinely fear an invasion of Manchuria' and that they would seek to establish a *cordon sanitaire* for border security 'regardless of the increased risk of general war'. On 24 November, as MacArthur lunged forward, the CIA found evidence to suggest a Chinese plan for 'major offensive operations'.

The best-informed media in the USA were strongly behind the march to the Yalu and just as incapable of judging Chinese intentions. A *New York Times* editorial claimed that it was incredible that China should feel threatened by 'a free and united Korea'; as the final offensive began, James Reston assured his readers that Washington sources did not think the Chinese would intervene, and an editorial lauded American forces for refusing to be 'deterred by Chinese communist threats'.

The Indian Ambassador to the People's Republic of China, K. M. Panikkar, consistently warned that the Chinese would not tolerate a march to the Yalu. On 25 September the Chinese Army's acting Chief of Staff, Nie Rongzhen, told him that China would have no option but to resist if the Americans continued to provoke them; when Panikkar said the experience of Korea had shown that the Americans would not spare 'a single industrial establishment' in China from bombing, Nie said that could not be helped. Zhou Enlai and the Polish Ambassador to Beijing said similar things, convincing Panikkar that China 'had decided on a more aggressive policy, regardless of [the] consequences'. A week later Zhou called him in

**An American chaplain
with his troops.**

and told him that China would not tolerate American soldiers crossing the parallel. But no one was listening because Panikkar was thought unreliable. Jessup and Rusk thought him 'temporarily following the Party line for ulterior motives'; his 'Mephistophelian quality', they wrote, 'was not limited to his spade beard'.

When the first contingents of Chinese volunteers entered Korea, Chinese sources cited the Korean volunteers in the Chinese civil war, likening them to Lafayette and his French soldiers in the American revolution and the Abraham Lincoln Brigade in the Spanish Civil War. 'We can never forget the Korean people . . . [who] participated not only in the war of liberation but also in the Northern expedition of 1925–7, in the land reform war of 1927–37 and in the anti-Japanese war of 1937–45.'

The principal reasons for the Chinese involvement would appear to be reciprocity first and the defence of the border next; of course, the two would mingle inextricably, reinforcing each other. A third important consideration would be the decisive supplanting of Soviet influence in North Korea.

US soldiers after Haktong battle in Northern Korea, 30 October 1950.

On 22 October American advisers had said that only scattered pockets of resistance were being encountered in the North; the Northern Army was no longer capable of an 'organized defence'. Within a few days, however, 'fresh, newly equipped North Korean troops' struck the UN front lines savagely with tanks and air support; ROKA units reeled back in disarray. Combined Sino-Korean units came roaring out of the mountains at Unsan, site of the old American gold-mine concession, on 26 October, and badly bloodied American forces; on the same day KPA attacks destroyed the ROK Army II Corps, thus crippling the right flank of the 8th Army. But shortly afterwards the enemy units disappeared again.

CIA daily reports this time caught the pattern of enemy rearward displacement, arguing that such withdrawals had in the past preceded offensive action and noting warily that there were 'large, coordinated and well-organized guerrilla forces in the rear area' behind the allied forces, along with guerrilla occupation of 'substantial areas in south-west Korea'. But as late as 20 November the estimate was still mixed, with some arguing that the communists were simply withdrawing to better defensive points

114

A South Korean minesweeper blows up in Wonsan harbour, 24 October 1950, the caption says on a Russian-type mine. It was to clear Wonsan harbour that the USA brought in Japanese Navy minesweepers and personnel – a fact that was covered up at the time. The Japanese admiral who commanded the operation said that this contribution by Japan was a key factor in persuading the USA to grant Japan its independence the following year.

and others that the pattern of 'giving ground invariably in face of UN units moving northward' merely meant 'a delaying action', not preparation for all-out assault.

From early November 1950 onwards MacArthur ordered that a wasteland be created between the front and the Chinese border, destroying from the air every 'installation, factory, city, and village' over thousands of square miles of North Korean territory. On 8 November seventy B–29s dropped 550 tons of incendiary bombs on Sinuiju, 'removing [it] from off the map'; a week later Hoeryong was hit with napalm 'to burn out the place'; by 25 November 'a large part of [the] North West [sic] area between Yalu river and southwards to enemy lines . . . [was] more or less burning'. Soon the area would be a 'wilderness of scorched earth'.

We may leave as an epitaph for this genocidal air war the views of its architect, General Curtis LeMay. After the war started, he said:

We slipped a note kind of under the door into the Pentagon and said, 'Look, let us go up there . . . and burn down five of the

Caption reads, 'En route to Chosin Reservoir. These prisoners, stragglers from North Korean units, are brought in by jeep trailer. Even the child was put to work, serving as an ammunition carrier, for the North Koreans.'

The first Chinese POWs in ▷ Hamhung, 30 October 1950.

American troops roll through the demolished town of Kapsan in November 1950, heartland of Kim Il Sung's guerrillas during the anti-Japanese resistance.

MacArthur lights his pipe as his plane runs up to the Yalu on the day of his fateful 'reconnaissance in depth', 24 November 1950.

biggest towns in North Korea – and they're not very big – and that ought to stop it.' Well, the answer to that was four or five screams – 'You'll kill a lot of non-combatants,' and 'It's too horrible.' Yet over a period of three years or so . . . we burned down *every* [sic] town in North Korea and South Korea, too . . . Now, over a period of three years this is palatable, but to kill a few people to stop this from happening – a lot of people can't stomach it.

On 24 November MacArthur launched his 'reconnaissance in force', a general offensive all along the line. He described it as a 'massive compression and envelopment', a 'pincer' movement designed to trap remaining Northern forces. On that day he flew over the Yalu, dipping the wings of his plane at American troops in Hyesanjin. The offensive rolled forward for three days against little or no resistance, ROK units succeeding in entering the important city of Chongjin. Lost amid the hoopla of American victory were reports from pilots that long columns of enemy troops were 'swarming all over the countryside'.

American soldiers enjoy a
Thanksgiving turkey
dinner on the banks of the
Yalu river, according to
the Signal Corps photo
caption.

# AN ENTIRELY NEW WAR

On 27 November 1950 Chinese and North Korean forces hit with devastating impact in a 'deep envelopment' that chopped the UN troops to pieces. The UN began a rapid retreat southwards. Observers wondered why they were moving so fast, often breaking contact with an enemy who was not necessarily pursuing them. On 15 December the British military attaché wrote, 'The withdrawal continues without any major enemy pressure'; there were no signs of defence lines being used to halt the enemy march. It looked like a 'phoney war', or a 'great hoax'.

In fact, the Chinese did not, in November and December, commit the enormous forces that Americans, then and since, have claimed. The total force was probably around 200,000. The shock effect of Chinese intervention was the critical element in destroying the US position. But the North Korean contribution, in both strategy and fighting power, was also important and has been completely underestimated. While Western sources were claiming that the North Koreans had been destroyed after Inchon, the People's Army put about 150,000 troops into the battles in November and December, as well as a large force of guerrillas. The evidence makes the indictment of MacArthur's generalship even more devastating. He not only ignored the palpable Chinese threat, but was also badly outmanoeuvred by the North Korean generals, who operated with a fraction of his *matériel*.

### Panic in Washington

In the last days of November 1950 panic gripped the government in Washington. The day after the Sino-Korean offensive began the situation was deemed capable of developing into 'complete involvement in total war'. US leaders sought to reverse their crushing defeat by contemplating the use of nearly every weapon in their arsenal.

On 30 November Truman rattled the atomic bomb in public. Asked at a press conference what steps he might take to stem the tide, he declined to rule out any measures and twice said that use of the bomb was under 'active consideration'. He then interrupted a question about whether this meant 'use against military objectives or civilian' to say that 'the military people' would decide that and narrowed this down to 'the military commander in the field', which meant MacArthur. His remarks were technically

**Refugees fleeing from Pyongyang across the tangled girders of a bridge over the River Taedong, 4 December 1950.**

121

wrong, as was pointed out in an instant White House 'clarification' (only the President can authorize use of the atomic bomb). He also said the USA would not wait for, or depend on, UN authorization. These remarks detonated a furore in Britain and threatened a split in the ruling Labour Party, which was particularly worried about MacArthur, especially since his unauthorized trip to Taiwan on 31 July. The remarks also caused great concern throughout much of Europe and the world. Britain's premier,

1949: Mao Zedong with his favourite son, Mao Anying, who was killed in Korea on 25 November 1950, apparently in a US bombing raid.

Peng Dehuai, Commander of the Chinese forces in Korea (the Chinese People's Volunteers), *left;* and Kim Il Sung, Commander-in-Chief of the Korean People's Army. Kim Il Sung is reported to have known Peng from the 1930s. Peng later became Defence Minister and was purged after standing up to Mao (the only top figure in China to do so). He died a gruesome death in 1974. Many of his colleagues in Korea now hold key positions at the top of the Chinese Army.

How a US comic portrayed the Chinese troops. The USA spoke of the Chinese as 'hordes' (leading one journalist to ask the US briefing officer, 'How many Chinese make up a horde?'). In fact, China put in far fewer troops than the USA suggested and often fought in small units.

Clement Attlee, hurried to Washington as the spokesman, in effect, not only for Britain but also for Europe and the Commonwealth.

At the time the USA had a strong advantage in atomic weaponry over the USSR: about 450 to twenty-five. Contrary to what is generally suggested, Truman's remarks were not a *faux pas*; they were a carefully weighed threat based on contingency planning to use the bomb. The crisis in Korea led to intense high-level discussions about the possible use of, or a threat to use, what Washington liked to call 'weapons of mass destruction': atomic and chemical weapons. On 30 November, the day of Truman's press conference, an order was issued that the Strategic Air Command be put on alert, 'to be prepared to dispatch without delay medium bomb groups to the Far East . . . this augmentation should include atomic capabilities'.

There was another possibility: to get out of Korea altogether. On 1 December 1950 a meeting was held at the Pentagon of the top figures

A neglected factor in the
defeat of the USA: Korean
guerrillas, seen here in a
North Korean photograph,
co-ordinating activities
with KPA regulars.

US soldiers surrendering, ▷
Pyongyang, December
1950. A Chinese officer
who was present told us
how this photograph was
taken. The US soldiers in
the picture did surrender
on this same spot, to
Chinese troops. But the
photograph was taken two
days later, when a film
unit was present. For
propaganda purposes a
North Korean soldier, who
had not been present at
the actual surrender, was
placed on one side.

in the administration except the President. The Joint Chiefs were split on the
value of Korea. CIA chief Bedell Smith recommended evacuation and said,
'We should get out of Korea, although we do not solve the problem by
getting out.'

Attlee arrived in Washington on 4 December, as UN forces
were retreating south under intense pressure and in bitter cold. Considerable disagreement emerged between the USA and Britain during several
days of talks.

The US participants said that it was unacceptable just to give
up, but since they had not done particularly well in Korea, maybe that was
not the best place to counter-attack. British Foreign Office records show that
the Americans pushed for a 'limited war' against China, including air
attacks, a blockade of the coast and covert introduction of anti-communist
forces in southern China. Attlee and the British spent more time arguing
against this plan than against the use of the A-bomb. Attlee argued against
turning China into an implacable enemy and sought a written promise that
the bomb would not be used in Korea. Truman would give him only oral
assurances.

Attlee's visit to Washington has often been presented (particularly in Britain) as a great victory for British moderation over American
extremism. Attlee's policy, especially on China, was moderate – and far-
sighted. But he acquired no real control over the use of the bomb. Immediately after he left Washington Truman secretly moved non-assembled
bombs to an aircraft-carrier off Korea and later, equally secretly, carried out
dummy nuclear runs over North Korea without informing the British
government. The Joint Chiefs of Staff, in a secret memorandum dated 12
January 1951, recommended expanding the war by unleashing the Kuomintang and 'giving such logistic support to those forces as will contribute to
effective operations against the Communists [in China]'.

US prisoners of war, ▷
winter 1950. Most US
deaths in captivity were
during this first winter.

One illuminating episode in the discussions came when the leaders were discussing how physically to evacuate Korea. They made a point of stressing that the plan must not leak to their Korean allies, who, it was felt, might turn and engage in guerrilla warfare against them on their way out.

The communist forces re-took Pyongyang on 5–6 December. Much of the city had been dynamited or burned by US, British and South Korean troops. The British liaison officer at MacArthur's headquarters reported back to London on what he called 'the unusual situation': US troops had had to fight their way *back* against guerrillas while being harried from the North.

The most decisive impact that guerrillas made was on the east coast. A large group of US Marines and soldiers was trapped near Lake Changjin (known in US parlance by its Japanese name, 'Frozen Chosin') where they were severely mauled by Chinese and North Korean units. American sources consider this the toughest battle of the war.

The UN forces in the North were divided: the 8th Army under General Walton H. Walker was on the west coast with British and Turkish units; on the east coast, separated by a high mountain range, was the X Corps under General Arnold. On the east coast the US forces, which included the Marines, fought courageously and effected an orderly withdrawal to the sea, receiving and inflicting high casualties. On the west coast British and Turkish forces resisted fiercely, but some US and ROK units retreated in disorderly manner, in what became known as 'bug out', abandoning equipment and, sometimes, the wounded. In addition, on the west side some UN forces broke contact with the more lightly armed enemy in a way that some participants and most observers consider was quite unnecessary.

From 3–10 December US military intelligence noted many reports of guerrilla flanking and envelopment movements south of the east coast port of Hungnam, for which the US troops were heading. The 'intense guerrilla activity which has occurred in these localities in the past three months' by regrouped North Korean units and guerrillas in the rear was now being coordinated with attacks by other Korean and Chinese units.

The rout of the US forces brought despondency to Washington. Dean Acheson later called it 'the worst defeat of US forces since Bull Run [in 1861]'. On 9 December Truman wrote, 'I've worked for peace for five years and six months and it looks like World War III is here. I hope not – but we must meet whatever comes – and we will.' Three days later he told the cabinet, 'We are faced with an all-out situation', with 'total mobilization' and the declaration of national emergency under consideration (it was brought in on 16 December). On 21 December MacArthur imposed full military censorship in Korea.

On 9 December MacArthur said that he desired commander's discretion to use atomic weapons. The day the US forces were pushed off the east coast he submitted 'a list of retardation targets' for which he needed

US troops retreat from
Lake Changjin ('Frozen
Chosin') towards
Hungnam, late 1950.

◁ Truman proclaiming a State of Emergency, 16 December 1950: 'Our homes, our Nation, all the things we believe in are in great danger . . . I summon our farmers, our workers in industry and our businessmen to make a mighty production effort to meet the defense requirements of the Nation and to this end to eliminate all waste and inefficiency and to subordinate all lesser interest to the common good.'

twenty-six atomic bombs. He also wanted four to drop on the 'invasion forces' and four more for 'critical concentrations of enemy air power'. In interviews published posthumously he said he had a plan that would have won the war in ten days: 'I would have dropped between thirty and fifty atomic bombs . . . strung across the neck of Manchuria.' Then he would have introduced half a million Chinese Nationalist troops at the Yalu and then 'spread behind us – from the Sea of Japan to the Yellow Sea – a belt of radioactive cobalt . . . it has an active life of between sixty and 120 years.' He expressed certainty that the Russians would have done nothing: 'My plan was a cinch.'

According to historian Carrol Quigley, cobalt 60 is 320 times as radioactive as radium. One 400-ton cobalt H-bomb could wipe out all animal life on earth. MacArthur sounds like a warmongering lunatic in these interviews, but, if so, he was not alone. Before the Sino-Korean offensive a committee of the Joint Chiefs had said that atomic bombs might be the 'decisive factor' in cutting off a communist advance into Korea; initially they could be useful in 'a *cordon sanitaire* [that] might be established by the UN in a strip immediately north of the Manchurian border'.

The record also shows that use of chemical weapons against Sino-North Korean forces was considered. In pencilled diary notes written on 16 December Ridgway referred cryptically to a subcommittee on the 'clandestine introduction [of] wea[pon]s of mass destruction and unconventional warfare'. We know nothing more about this item, but it may refer to an apparent request put by him to MacArthur that chemical weapons be used. The original of Ridgway's telegram is unavailable, but MacArthur's reply, on 7 January 1951, read: 'I do not believe there is any chance of using chemicals on the enemy in case evacuation is ordered. As you know, US inhibitions on such use are complete and drastic . . .' The next day, in a conference with General Almond and others, the transcript says, 'If we use gas we will lay ourselves open to retaliation. This question has been taken up with General MacArthur for decision. We have requested sufficient quantities to be shipped immediately in the event use of gas is approved.'

**Blowing up the port of Hungnam, North Korea, 24 December 1950. The UN forces had to get out by sea because of the guerrillas south of Hungnam. The port was blown up by the USA at least partly out of revenge for its crushing defeat at Lake Changjin a few weeks earlier.**

**The monster 'Tarzon' bomb, 21 feet high and weighing 12,000 pounds, that was first tried out in Korea at the end of 1950, during the retreat from the North. It had fins for guidance but was quite inaccurate; although it inflicted enormous damage, it was not considered a success and was discontinued.**

The Chinese (PRC) delegation at the UN (First Committee meeting), 27 November 1950. The head of the Chinese delegation, General Wu Xiuquan, is on the left, with future Foreign Minister Qiao Guanhua behind him; Britain's delegate, Kenneth Younger, *centre*; John Foster Dulles, *right*. Although the PRC had been denied China's seat at the UN, the UN was forced to allow this delegation to attend for a short time. The Chinese delegation appeared at the UN just as Chinese troops were inflicting severe defeats on the US forces in Korea.

Hooded prisoners, Seoul, ▷ December 1950.

In the meantime the USA pounded the North with conventional air power. On 14–15 December the Air Force hit Pyongyang with 700 500-lb bombs, napalm and 175 tons of delayed-fuse demolition bombs. These were timed to blow up at odd moments up to seventy-two hours after they landed, causing maximum insecurity and multiplying casualties among people trying to rescue the dead or to escape from the napalm fires. At about the same time American B–29s dropped 'Tarzon' bombs on Kanggye.

## The Communist Advance

For the Chinese, entry into the war was costly in terms of both manpower and funds. Casualties among the Chinese troops were very high in the first winter, which was exceptionally cold. The Chinese 9th Army alone was estimated to have lost 45,000 dead in the period 27 November to 12 December. One Chinese soldier told us that during this first winter they often had to sleep out in the open, in minus 30 degrees Centigrade, without blankets. It was so cold that they could not sleep lying down but had to rest in a sitting position. They could not light fires because of the US planes. Ears, noses, fingers and toes often dropped off at a mere touch. But China's troops were also doing very well against the USA. Acheson later wrote to Truman: 'The defeat of the US forces in Korea in December [1950] was an incalculable defeat to US foreign policy.' This conditioned the spirit of the US Army and the political debate within the USA, and gave China increased international prestige.

As for the USSR, the weight of the evidence is that it was not happy about the war. North Korean sources have indicated in private that they were extremely bitter about the slowness and meagre quantities of

South Korean vigilantes ▷ guarding prisoners during the UN retreat, Sariwon, North Korea, 6 December 1950.

130

Soviet aid in the initial period of the war. The strongest evidence that Soviet aid was absolutely minimal comes from General MacArthur himself. While the Western governments were claiming that the USSR had armed North Korea to the teeth and triggered off the war, the Australian diplomat James Plimsoll reported MacArthur as saying (in late November 1950), 'No evidence had been found of any close connection between the Soviet Union and the North Korean aggression . . . MacArthur thought that if it had really inspired the North Korean aggression, the Soviet Union would not have abandoned the North Koreans so completely, giving them no assistance whatever. "This [said MacArthur] would have been the greatest betrayal in history since Judas accepted his thirty pieces of silver."'

In autumn 1950 the Soviet Union moved planes into northeast China. The first MIG appeared on 1 November 1950. Colonel G. K. Plotnikov later confirmed to us in 1987 that Soviet pilots flew MIGs in combat against the Americans in Korea. The Russians flew only over the northern part of North Korea, usually only as far south as the Chongchon river or, at maximum, Pyongyang. They were not allowed to cross the thirty-eighth parallel or fly over the sea (where it would be much easier for the Americans to capture them if they were shot down). The Russians have claimed in print to have shot down 'tens' of US planes. Soviet sources told us that the commander of their air force in Korea, G. A. Lobov, shot down fourteen US planes. But they also suffered heavy losses. One claim that the Russians made to us was that the USA used German pilots in Korea, presumably because they had combat experience of flying against Soviet fliers.

The Russians also say that they prepared five divisions of the Red Army to help North Korea 'to resist aggression' – presumably meaning if the USA tried to push too far north again. US sources claim that the Russians stationed troops in North Korea. Senior Soviet sources strongly denied this to us. Soviet military aid increased considerably from 1951.

By late December 1950 the North Koreans had re-taken the territory they had held as of 25 June. Communist forces crossed the thirty-eighth parallel into the South on 26 December 1950.

In late December 1950 the ruling Workers' Party met at the town of Kanggye. Its first task was to restore the administration on this blasted wasteland. The regime was concerned about the loyalty of the population. The restoration of power in maximally adverse conditions was extremely fraught. It is significant, though, that there were no important defections from the party to the other side, throughout the war, even though many members came fom the South.

As the communist forces approached the thirty-eighth parallel the USA considered doing what the British called 'a Dunkirk' and abandoning the peninsula completely.

There was renewed panic in the Rhee regime as the communists approached. Executions of political foes and prisoners were speeded up. On 15 December police carried out a mass execution of prisoners –

Relatives remove bodies
from the site of a North
Korean atrocity committed
at Chonju, September 1950.

South Korea, 16 January
1951. The original caption
reads, 'US soldier fighting
sniper in house'.

A village in the South, 22
January 1951. The caption
says, 'Whole villages are
losing their men in a mass
voluntary move to get
organized and into action
against the communists.
American Military Police
and Republic of Korea
Police help to organize the
recruits for the Southern
Army.' This was the point
of maximum Chinese–
North Korean advance,
and the South was
desperate to restock its
depleted army.

134

A bloodstained cell in a jail in Nampo, North Korea, as photographed by the US Army Signal Corps, October 1950.

which was witnessed by some British troops. The report from Britain's man in Seoul, Alec Adams, read:

> As I understand it, considerable feeling was aroused among British troops both because of the callous way in which the executions were carried out and because they mistook two of those shot for boys (they were in fact women wearing trousers). Fearing that there would be an incident if British troops were again subjected [*sic*] to the spectacle of mass executions in their vicinity, I represented to the United States Embassy yesterday the urgent need to dissuade the Korean authorities from running unnecessary risks.

On 17 December another mass execution took place, but this time there was no problem – British (and US) troops were kept well away. The tenor of the times and the shallowness of the British Labour government's concern are shown by the Foreign Office documents. J. S. H. Shattock at the Foreign Office wrote to Adams in Seoul: 'The continuing reports of "atrocities" and "political shootings" are, as you know, giving us a lot of trouble . . . we are indeed sorry to have to burden you with these requests for information.' A few days later all is well; a Foreign Office official writes on the report: 'Public interest in the executions seems to have abated and we do not expect much further trouble.' ('Trouble' here, of course, refers not to Rhee's executions, many of which were carried out after torture, but to irritating questions in Britain.) Adams had earlier cabled the Foreign Office to say that 'even by reading between the lines' it was hard to imagine the brutality of the regime.

North Korea, May 1951: members of the International Women's Federation at the site of an atrocity carried out during UN occupation.

137

Man and child in the ruins
of Sunuiju, May 1951.
This city, on the Korean
side of the Yalu, was a
particular target of US
bombing, as the key
railway bridge from China
was here. This destruction
is less than one-third of
the way into the war.

A Canadian soldier,
Corporal Andy Dore,
somewhere in Korea, 28
June 1951.

Grief-stricken
North Korean
woman at
massacre site,
May 1951.
Note the
blasted
landscape.

This was not the only problem for the UN side. Was there a Southern army to stem the communist advance? And who was in charge of it?

The commander of the 8th Army, General Walker, had been killed on 23 December. He was replaced by General Matthew Ridgway, who has given an evocative description of the situation he confronted on assuming the job:

> On New Year's morning I drove out north of Seoul and into a dismaying spectacle. ROK soldiers by truckloads were streaming south, without orders, without arms, without leaders, in full retreat . . . They had just one aim – to get as far away from the Chinese as possible. They had thrown away their rifles and pistols and had abandoned all artillery, mortars, machine-guns, every crew-served weapon . . .
>
> I leaped out of my jeep and stood in the middle of the road waving my arms over my head to flag down an approaching truck. The first few dodged by me without slowing down but I did soon succeed in stopping a group of trucks all carrying ROK officers. The group in the advance truck listened without comprehension and would not obey my gestures. Soon the whole procession was rolling again. The only effective move now was to set up straggler posts far to the rear, manned by our

*Massacre in Korea* by
**Picasso, painted in 1951.**

*From left:* **Pak Chong-ae (head of women's organization), Ho Chong-suk (Minister of Health), Kim Il Sung and Pak Hon-yong (Foreign Minister) at a meeting welcoming the International Women's Federation delegation, Pyongyang, May 1951. Pak Hon-yong, the leader of the Southern communists, was executed on trumped-up charges when the war ended.**

own MPs . . . to try to regain control. This method worked. The routed forces were reorganized into units . . .

Several months later Army Chief of Staff General Collins told the US Congress: 'Every time they [the South Koreans] are hit by the Chinamen they just plain run.' General Bradley, chairman of the US Joint Chiefs of Staff, told the same Congressional hearings that the South Korean Army had then, eleven months into the war, lost the equivalent of ten divisions of equipment.

The USA continued to blow up cities and installations on its retreat within the South. The port city of Inchon was, in the words of one US source, 'destroyed by UN forces' as they pulled out on 3 January 1951. Much of Seoul was also put to the torch by UN troops. The USA marked its abandonment of Seoul with a massive air raid on Pyongyang on 3 January.

Somewhat later Ridgway had second thoughts about the firing of towns, telling one of his commanders, 'I have been struck by those areas I have visited which had formerly been occupied by the CCF [Chinese]. There appeared to have been little or no vandalism committed . . . You have my full authority [to safeguard your troops] . . . this does not, however, extend to the wanton destruction of towns and villages, by gunfire or bomb, unless there is good reason to believe them occupied.'

**Refugees**

By now Seoul was a shattered, frozen and largely ruined prize. Much of the population had left. The city had changed hands three times within barely six months.

Refugees trudging through
deep snow near
Kangnung, 8 January 1951.

Controversy seethes over the movements of population. Western sources usually claim that hundreds of thousands of people, even millions, 'voted with their feet' and fled from the North to the South. North Korean sources claim that many people fled in the opposite direction. They acknowledge that considerable numbers of people went south but say that they were either forcibly removed by the Americans and South Koreans or terrorized by the prospect of the A-bomb and other threats.

No one knows how many people moved or why they did. What can safely be said is that many people did flee voluntarily from North to South, particularly Christians. Their motives for fleeing ranged from outright anti-communism to fear of reprisals, via a desire to rejoin relatives in the South. Numbers of others moved South because of fear or out of straightforward concern for safety, motives that in all honesty can hardly be called 'voluntary'. There is evidence that people in the North genuinely feared that they might be hit with atomic weapons. US unit reports also record deporting all military-age males in their areas to the South. What is not open to doubt is that US bombing was a key factor in many people's decision to move.

The only place where civilians could feel safe was behind the lines of the side doing the bombing. One important fact rarely mentioned is that over half the population of Seoul fled when the UN forces were approaching in September 1950. No one in the West suggests this was because they 'voted with their feet' against Rhee (although this may well have been a reason).

Many people did want to flee from the communists. The re-imposition of communist rule in the winter of 1950–51 was harsh. The returning administration was distrustful of the loyalty of the population in the areas that had been occupied by the UN and Rhee's officials and police. Many people were executed, imprisoned or subjected to various forms of isolation and ostracism. Many were fearful that the returning regime would engage in reprisals – and it often did. One reason why we know this is because senior officials, including Kim Chaek, issued orders to stop the killings. Another rarely mentioned reason why some people fled south-wards was fear of the Chinese – more because they were an unknown quantity than because people actually knew anything about them (in fact, they behaved scrupulously towards the local population). But any-one who has seen pictures of the North as it was in the winter of 1950–51 and the destruction of Hungnam (or Inchon), with temperatures falling to minus 40 degrees Centigrade, with food stocks burned, animals slaughtered and entire villages razed to the ground, might reconsider why people moved.

The UN sometimes also created refugees. The US magazine *Christian Century* described how South Korean police would force people out of their homes to make it easier to loot them, as well as to increase the 'head count'. The BBC's correspondent René Cutforth suggested another reason when he wrote of 'the horrible brutality and corruption of Syngman Rhee's police, among whose chief rackets was the selling of destitute girls from the refugee columns into the city brothels'.

Seoul was not a safe place to be in January 1951. But it was not a safe place to leave either. As people fled across the frozen Han river, South Korean police shot their bullocks and turned their guns on the civilians, then troops mortared the ice in front of the refugees to prevent them from getting across. This scene was witnessed by Cutforth, one of the most honest Western correspondents – but he did not mention it at the time on the BBC.

In the first few weeks of January the communist forces pushed south of Seoul for about 60 miles, roughly to the thirty-seventh parallel. By now they were some 200 miles from China. China itself at this point probably had about 400,000 troops in the field. The logistics of supplying this army were mind-boggling. It is estimated that some 700,000 troops and porters were involved in carrying supplies, largely on their backs, from China to the front. The USA had complete control of the air: everyone and everything that moved was subjected to constant bombing and strafing. People could move only at night, which was also the only time when repairs could be carried out to bridges, railways and roads – all made far more dangerous by delayed-action bombs.

There was also the problem of actually acquiring the military hardware in the first place. Chinese and North Korean troops often made bayonet charges on heavily armed UN positions. Most communist troops did not have helmets but went into battle wearing only soft caps. An East European surgeon who worked in a North Korean Army hospital told us that head injuries, many of them fatal, were very extensive as a result.

On 25 January 1951 the communists launched a new offensive, which was checked. Their advance had reached its maximum feasible extent in logistical terms. Ridgway's morale-stiffening efforts had also begun to work. At this point the tide turned.

Peng Dehuai, the commander of the Chinese forces, went back to China to tell Mao that the war could not be won. The supply lines were at their maximum viable length. Chinese sources have suggested that it was never their intention to try to push the USA out of Korea completely and have indicated, plausibly, that this was a political calculation: if the USA had been ejected it might well have struck back directly at China. It would seem that China's goal was to push the USA and Rhee back into the South and settle for that.

By the end of February UN forces were back on the Han river, just south of Seoul. The USA blasted the capital. One of the people watching was a young man named Samuel Cohen, on a secret assignment for the US Defense Department. He thought that there must be a way to destroy the enemy without destroying the city. He later became the father of the neutron bomb. On 14 March the communists evacuated Seoul with heavy losses. UN forces soon re-crossed the thirty-eighth parallel, advancing north of Taepo-ri on the east coast by late April.

The power of napalm: on a
hilltop and on a factory.

### Political Questions in the Civil War

The political character of the war is rarely addressed. In its early phases there was a political struggle – to gain adherents and to eliminate enemies. From about the time of the entry of the Chinese forces in late 1950, the character of the war changed.

Although the North Koreans could not reach across the battle line in the same way as the Vietnamese revolution did, this does not mean that the war was simply a 'front-line' war. Guerrillas played a big role. Nor does it mean that Rhee acquired any greater popularity or legitimacy than before. Cutforth summed up the activity of his forces in this period as 'plenty of massacres, not much fighting'. A US Embassy official wrote that 'probably more than 100,000' people were killed by Rhee officials in the South after his regime was re-imposed by MacArthur in September 1950. This is a far higher figure than the maximum US claim for all people murdered by the communists in North and South during the whole war. No one knows how many people were killed by Rhee later on. One of the few cases of mass execution that reached the Western press (and was universally accepted as having been carried out by his forces) took place in February 1951 in Kochang, in the South. There some 600 civilians, women, children and men, were herded into a ditch and mown down by machine-gun fire – on the grounds solely of being suspected of being communists.

Guerrilla warfare was the most important factor characterizing the nature of the conflict. Many weeks after the Inchon landing, MacArthur reported: 'Communist guerrilla units varying from a few hundred to several thousand men are operating in isolated areas throughout the United Nations occupied portion of Korea. At present, nearly 30 per cent of the United Nations troops in Korea are employed against them in . . . protecting supply lines and the more vital urban centres.' MacArthur estimated guerrilla strength at between 30,000 and 35,000. A well-informed US military source says that guerrilla activity increased after that to a peak in mid-January 1951: 'The attacks, which invariably surprised the defenders, were based on detailed target information, meticulously planned and executed with split-second timing.' They were 'frequently noted in the rear of the most active sectors of the UN front'.

Most Western sources suggest that the guerrillas were a short-lived phenomenon that soon dwindled away. This is not true. The official US military history states that in late 1950 'enemy guerrilla action . . . extended all the way to the southern tip of Korea'. Guerrillas were harassing the railways in central Korea and even seized medium-sized towns. Ridgway moved to wipe them out towards the end of 1951 with 'Operation Ratkiller'. By the end of January 1952, according to Ridgway, the operation had succeeded: 'Nearly 20,000 freebooters – bandits and organized guerrillas – had been killed or captured, and the irritation was ended for good.' Most of the guerrillas were in the Chiri mountains in south-west Korea, but there were some in other areas. Stanley Weintraub records that guerrillas

Margaret Bourke-White reports on what she called 'the savage, secret war' in the Cholla provinces in South-west Korea, 1952.

Trussed guerrilla being brought in dead.

were able to kill a top US officer and others outside his office near Pusan in mid-1952. Nor were the strongholds in the Chiri mountains wiped out, as Ridgway claimed, by January 1952. The photographer Margaret Bourke-White did a feature for *Life* magazine in December 1952 entitled 'The savage, secret war in Korea', in which she described a powerful guerrilla force – which included many women – still highly active in mid-1952: 'Some of the guerrillas are converts who went over to the Reds in their first great offens-

The caption reads, 'Captured women guerrillas are judged as harshly as men. Most of these face five- to ten-year jail sentences. But some of them will be shot.'

Police chief Han celebrates victory. The caption says that he 'regales his men and "Kisaeng girls" (Korean *geishas*) with popular Japanese song, "China Night"'.

ive. Thousands of others are North Koreans bypassed in the UN breakout from the Pusan perimeter. Others have filtered South through Allied lines' – in other words, a composite force that could hardly have survived for two years, in harsh mountain conditions and in the middle of generalized warfare, without some substantial local support.

Command of 'Operation Ratkiller' was assigned to one of South Korea's toughest and most anti-communist officers, General Paek Sun-yop. No one can compute what really happened in the campaign. A footnote in the official US history hints bleakly at one possibility:

> Although there were reportedly only 8,000 guerrillas in south-western Korea before RATKILLER and supposedly over 9,000 were killed and captured during the operation, Ridgway's headquarters estimated in March [1952] that there were still over 3,000 guerrillas left in the area. Either there were far more guerrillas to begin with or a great many innocent bystanders were caught up in the dragnet.

The Southern regime was not able to show any such support in the North, in spite of overwhelming technical superiority (control of the sea, helicopters and the possibility of parachuting in agents, none of which was available to the North). There was also a much larger campaign than has generally been recognized to try to promote guerrilla activity in the communist-held area. The senior British officer involved, Major W. Ellery Anderson, described to us the inability of a US–British team, with Korean

ROK General Paek Sun-yop, in charge of anti-guerrilla campaign 'Operation Ratkiller', looking at map with US officer, 30 December 1951. Although many thousands of alleged guerrillas were killed and captured, the guerrillas were not wiped out.

A South Korean agent (originally from the North) dressed up as a North Korean security official before being parachuted into the North with British and American special forces. UN guerrilla operations in the North were not successful.

Koje: a burning village, summer 1952. The USA removed the villagers and burned their houses because they were helping the POWs.

Three men hanged as spies in the North. The Soviet correspondent who took this picture told us that the three men had been parachuted into the North disguised as KPA and had been caught in Pyongyang driving the wrong type of jeep for their rank. When the men were brought to the gallows an appeal was made for volunteers to carry out the execution; large numbers of people rushed forward to offer their services.

North Korean Self-Defence Force women.

agents, to stir up anything in the North in 1951–2. The population of the North, he told us, 'just didn't want to know'. In addition, the Americans and British ran sizeable sabotage and intelligence-gathering parties from islands off the two coasts for long periods.

Gen. Charles Willoughby (MacArthur's intelligence chief), Gen. Ridgway (Commander, 8th Army) and Walter Bedell Smith, Taegu, Korea, 17 January 1951. Smith, known as 'the toughest ass-chewer in the US Army', was appointed head of the CIA in October 1950. Willoughby is looking anxious – with good reason. Smith's mission was to wrest control over intelligence away from Willoughby, an unreliable character.

MacArthur and Ridgway, ▷ Seoul, 24 March 1951 (Gen. Whitney behind). This was MacArthur's penultimate visit, less than three weeks before he was fired. After his sacking, MacArthur told the US Congress, 'The war in Korea has almost destroyed that nation. I have never seen such devastation. I have seen, I guess, as much blood and disaster as any living man, and it just curdled my stomach the last time I was there. After I looked at that wreckage and those thousands of women and children and everything, I vomited . . . If you go on indefinitely, you are perpetuating a slaughter such as I have never heard of in the history of mankind.' The devastation that MacArthur saw was a quarter of the way into the war – and not in the most shattered part of Korea.

## Truman Fires MacArthur

As the communists drove South, MacArthur appeared to suggest that he would actually welcome being pushed off the Korean peninsula, as this would make it easier to go straight for China.

In mid-January 1951 a top-level US mission went to Tokyo to confer with him. It included General J. Lawton Collins, the Army Chief of Staff; General Hoyt Vandenberg, the Air Force Chief of Staff; and CIA chief Walter Bedell Smith. After the conference Collins announced that UN forces would 'certainly stay in Korea and fight', and the commander of the Far East Air Force's Bomber Command, Major-General Emmett O'Donnell, was relieved of his command. Like MacArthur, he had been an advocate of carrying the war to China, preferably with atomic weapons.

For China, however, it may not always have been clear what 'the American government' was. As far as it could see, it might be attacked by American forces, whether directed by MacArthur or not. The rapidly expanding CIA was stepping up raids on the Chinese mainland. On 1 February 1951 the USA applied intense pressure to push through the UN a resolution condemning China as an 'aggressor'. It was essentially because of this resolution that China was deprived of a seat in the UN for a further two decades. It was the Korean war, not the Chinese civil war, that led to both the freezing of the division of China and the exclusion of the People's Republic from the UN.

US policy-making was treading a razor's edge over atomic weapons. It would seem that the USA came closest to using them in early

A wounded Chinese
soldier receiving treatment
from a UN medic, 9 March
1951.

spring 1951. On 10 March MacArthur asked for something he called a '"D" Day atomic capability'. At the end of March atomic-bomb-loading pits on Okinawa were operational; the bombs were ostensibly carried there unassembled and put together at the base. It is not clear whether the bombs were assembled and ready for use. But on 5 April the Joint Chiefs ordered immediate atomic retaliation against Manchurian bases if large numbers of new troops came into the fighting, or, it appears, if bombers were launched from there against American forces; and on 6 April Truman issued an order approving the Joint Chiefs' request and the transfer of a limited number of complete atomic weapons 'to military custody'.

Meanwhile tension between MacArthur and Washington had escalated. There were two basic issues at stake. One was the matter of attacking China. The second was the manner in which MacArthur tried to get his way, which amounted to insubordination. If China was to be attacked, Truman did not want MacArthur in the lead because he could not control the general. It was on this latter ground that MacArthur was dismissed on 11 April 1951. One result was that Truman's 6 April order was never sent.

The dismissal of MacArthur was greeted with relief by most of the USA's allies and with dismay by Chiang Kai-shek and much of US public opinion. MacArthur's successor as Supreme Commander was General Matthew Ridgway, his place as Commander of the 8th Army being taken by General James Van Fleet, who got the job because he had just successfully crushed the partisan army in Greece.

On the ground the UN was now north of the thirty-eighth parallel again across most of the peninsula. The communist forces struck back. From 22 April to 22 May there was bitter see-saw fighting on a gigantic scale. Peng Dehuai says that 1 million men took part on each side. US estimates are lower: 542,000 Chinese plus 197,000 North Koreans on one side, 240,000 South Koreans plus 270,000 US forces and allies on the other.

The communist armies once again reached the edge of Seoul, which seems to have been their goal. They made a point of going for the South Koreans, with conspicuous success: there was 'a complete fold-up' of the South Korean 6th Division.

US forces counter-attacked and by 24 June had pushed back on average about 25 miles along the entire front, so that the new battle line lay mainly north of the thirty-eighth parallel, except in the far west. The UN took almost 10,000 prisoners, the vast majority of them Chinese.

While the war on the ground reached relative stalemate by early summer 1951, there was another important side to the conflict: the bombing of the North from the air and the bombardment of the coastal areas from the sea continued unabated.

The virtually unhindered war from the sea has generally been ignored. During the heavy fighting in early 1951, for example, three cities on the east coast, Wonsan, Songjin and Chongjin, were blasted. Strict censorship – the strictest of the war, according to I. F. Stone – shrouded the

**US soldiers escort the mayor of Chipyong-ni (wearing traditional *yangban* dress) and his wife (slumped beside him), 18 May 1951. The caption says that the mayor had refused to leave.**

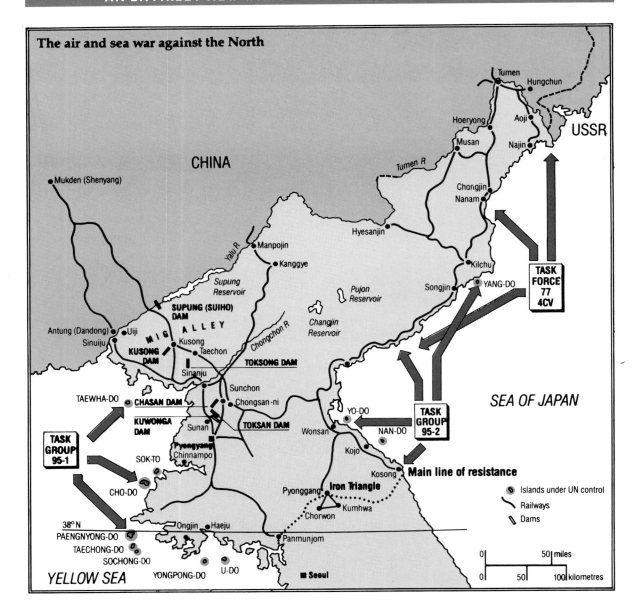

The air and sea war against the North

episode. On 29 March Rear-Admiral Allan F. Smith said that UN ships had been bombarding Wonsan for forty-one 'straight days and nights . . . the longest sustained naval or air bombardment of a city in history'. He described life in the city, the largest on the east coast: 'In Wonsan you cannot walk in the streets. You cannot sleep anywhere in the twenty-four hours, unless it is the sleep of death.' Smith said the UN fleet had reduced the population to 'suicide groups' and that Songjin and Chongjin were being given the same treatment. An international delegation of women visiting Wonsan a few weeks later found appalling devastation.

156

According to the official US Navy history, the siege of Wonsan was 'the longest in modern American naval history'. It lasted 861 days and finished one minute before the ceasefire hour of 10 p.m. on 27 July 1953. By then, according to the US history, Wonsan was 'a mass of cluttered ruins . . . Hardly an undamaged building was visible. Many industries had gone underground.'

Control of the sea also meant that the USA could threaten another 'Inchon'. The USA prepared a number of major amphibious landings, some of them as feints, but in at least one case with the intention of a possible landing if conditions proved suitable. It was estimated that at a peak some 60,000 communist troops were tied down by these landing threats in 1951.

△

**The Gloucester pub, London; the sign commemorates a battle on the Imjin river in April 1951, when a British battalion, the Gloucesters, staged a delaying action against Chinese forces.**

**Part of the city of Wonsan at the end of the war. The city was under uninterrupted siege for 861 days.**

# 5

# TALKING WHILE FIGHTING

### Peace Talks – and More Pressure

Secret talks at the end of May and in early June 1951, between the Soviet Ambassador to the UN, Jacob Malik, and the US diplomat George Kennan, brought about a US–Soviet understanding on the advisability of talks in the field. During a radio broadcast on 23 June Malik called for 'a ceasefire and an armistice providing for the mutual withdrawal of forces from the thirty-eighth parallel'. His proposal was taken up with alacrity.

This phase of the war was one of continued heavy land fighting rather like that in the First World War: heavy use of artillery, with both sides dug into well-entrenched defensive positions. Ground could be taken only at very high cost in either ammunition or human life or both.

The failure of the last big Chinese offensive, the '5th Campaign', in early summer 1951 had convinced the communist side that further major advances were out of the question, short of sacrificing immense numbers of lives and, even then, logistically probably impossible. Equally the UN side, having recovered territory slightly more extensive than that lying below the thirty-eighth parallel, was ready to consider a draw. This outcome was all the more appealing as the question of casualties was becoming an issue, particularly in the USA. What American commanders often referred to as 'real estate' could now be acquired only with unacceptable levels of dead and wounded. Wilfred Bacchus's study, 'The Relationship between Combat and Peace Negotiations . . . in Korea', states flatly, 'It was the increase in casualties that had the greatest impact on the conduct of the war, once the truce talks had begun.'

The year and a half between the opening of truce talks and the accession of Eisenhower to the US presidency saw the war shift to a different pattern: on the military front, heavy ground fighting for limited objectives along a basically stable front line, while the UN deployed superior air power to limit communist capability at the battle line; on the political front, the communists tried to use the talks to seize the initiative, wear down the West and, when possible, spring disconcerting surprises, like POW rebellions and confessions by US airmen, to tilt the balance of advantage to their own side.

The UN went into the peace talks with a commanding lead not only in air and naval power but also in numbers of troops: 550,000 compared with 460,000 on the communist side. But this did not hold for

**North Korean troops.**

159

long. UN casualties more than trebled in heavy fighting in September and October 1951 in battles like 'Heartbreak Ridge' (Height 1211), which the North Koreans consider their single toughest battle of the war. During the same period enemy losses only doubled, reducing the ratio of losses from about 20:1 to about 14:1, falling slightly further towards the end of 1951. At the same time the communists managed to increase their forces and overtake the UN: by December 1951 the Chinese–North Korean forces totalled 800,000 men compared with 600,000 for the UN. One year later the UN had closed the gap slightly, fielding 768,000 to the communists' 900,000.

This period saw bitter fighting: battles that became famous in the West for places christened 'Heartbreak Ridge', 'Old Baldy', 'Porkchop Hill', 'White Horse Hill' (Hill 395), 'Jackson Heights', 'Triangle Hill' (Hill 598) – even 'Jane Russell Hill'. Each of these caused high casualties. But none of them was militarily decisive, and this fact became known and itself was a factor that pushed the politicians towards ending the war.

In early June US Defense Secretary Marshall visited Korea for six hours to inform the field commanders about the upcoming talks. He told Ridgway that conditions in Korea were worse than he had realized and is reported to have said that he would recommend to Truman that they tell the Chinese leaders, whom he knew well, that unless the fighting stopped 'we are going to give them a taste of the atom'. In his memoirs China's Marshal Nie Rongzhen says 'most' of China's leaders were in favour of negotiations at this point and that it was in June 1951 that Mao issued the key directive to go over to 'active defence'. Nie implies that the North Koreans were more reluctant to begin talks.

Talks opened at the town of Kaesong, just below the thirty-eighth parallel, on 10 July. The communist side was represented by a joint North Korean–Chinese delegation, while the UN side was represented by US officers, with one ROK associate.

These negotiations were an immense breakthrough for North Korea and China. The USA had refused to recognize them diplomatically and even politically. Evoking the atmosphere, the Hungarian journalist Tibor Meray said: 'You had to see how Nam Il walked into the negotiating tent. You had to see how the communist delegates moved, how they sat. They had been denied recognition. But these talks *were* recognition.'

This was a double psychological victory: over the USA because Americans were negotiating with people they did not 'recognize' and over the South Koreans, who were subordinate to the USA.

The talks got off to a cracking start. By 26 July an agenda had been agreed. Major disputes arose over accusations that both sides had violated the demilitarized area agreed for the talks, and negotiations were several times broken off on these grounds. Early on in the talks a Chinese unit marched through the demilitarized area armed with machine-guns and 60-mm mortars. The Chinese said that the unit was a company of Military Police and that the march was a 'mistake'. In September 1951 a US plane strafed Kaesong: the USA said it was a 'mistake'. The communists many

A North Korean woman soldier with an American helicopter pilot at Kaesong, 8 July 1951, the first day on which liaison teams from the two sides met to discuss peace talks, which opened on 10 July.

times charged that the USA had bombed and strafed the neutral area and the communist negotiating team, both inside the neutral area and *en route* to it. It was claimed that these were deliberate attempts by sectors of the US military to sabotage the talks at key moments – and possibly to assassinate communist delegates. At the time the USA denied most of the charges. The official US military history later acknowledged that the USA carried out a large number of violations, including strafing and bombing the neutral zone and bombing the communist negotiators' convoy *en route* to the talks. Describing reported violations in spring 1952, the official history says laconically: 'While the UNC [United Nations Command] representatives denied responsibility for *some* of these accusations, there were enough infractions to place the UNC delegation *constantly* on the defensive' [authors' emphasis]. When a Western reporter asked the chief US briefing officer about one of these strafing episodes, the officer replied, 'Don't you forget which side you're on.'

An intense propaganda war surrounded the talks. Phillip Knightley has described the UN's public relations in these words:

> Since the [Western] correspondents were apparently not prepared to back the war wholeheartedly and without reservation, censorship at the peace talks became total. Correspondents accredited to the United Nations Command were forbidden to speak with the UN negotiators . . . [They] were prohibited from

inspecting documents presented at the negotiations and were allowed to see only those maps specially prepared for them by the United States Army's public relations section. The picture the correspondents received in this manner – and which they faithfully reported to their public – was a mixture of lies, half-truths, and serious distortions.

To the consternation of the USA the communist side proved rather skilful at public relations and is generally considered to have come out ahead. Two Western journalists, Alan Winnington and Wilfred Burchett, played a major role in making the communist negotiating position known to the world. One key episode occurred early on in the talks, when the USA claimed that it was offering an armistice line corresponding to the actual battle line, though, in fact, it was demanding a line considerably further to the north; it also claimed that the communists were refusing an armistice line along the actual battle line, when in fact the communists had proposed this. Burchett and Winnington exposed this deception – with considerable impact. They did such a good job that Ridgway tried to ban 'fraternization' but had to abandon the attempt after a press revolt.

The USA also exerted pressure by means of direct activities against China. It bombed the main city on the Chinese side of the Yalu,

**The North Korean–Chinese negotiating team, Kaesong, 16 July 1951, a few days after full-scale talks began.** *From left:* **Maj.-Gen. Xie Fang (CPV), Lt-Gen. Deng Hua (CPV), Gen. Nam Il (KPA), Maj.-Gen. Li Sang Cho (KPA), Maj-Gen. Chang Pyong San (KPA). General Nam Il headed the Korean–Chinese team throughout the talks. Deng Hua had been the head of the Special Standing-by Unit of the Chinese Army set up in August 1950 to prepare to go into Korea.**

The UN negotiating team, Kaesong, 16 July 1951. *Front row from left:* Maj.-Gen. Laurence C. Craigie (USA); Gen. Paek Sun-yop (ROKA); Admiral C. Turner Joy (USA); Maj.-Gen. Henry Hodes (USA); Admiral Arleigh Burke (US Navy). The USA negotiated alone for its allies. Joy was replaced as head of the UN team in May 1952 by Army Lt-Gen. William K. Harrison.

Dandong, and stepped up clandestine missions into the mainland. There was a huge expansion of the CIA during the Korean war, with a heavy emphasis on subversion and sabotage. China was number one target. A former CIA agent has written that the CIA 'was at this time also supporting an attempt to invade communist China'. Ray Cline, a key CIA operative in Taiwan, has described one of the CIA's tasks at the time as 'to support paramilitary efforts to impede the Chinese fighting in Korea by preventing communist consolidation of its control over all of mainland China'.

Another important development concerned atomic weapons. The first tests of tactical nuclear weapons had been held in January 1951. In June that year the Joint Chiefs again considered using the bomb, this time in tactical battlefield circumstances. Robert Oppenheimer was involved in 'Project Vista', designed to gauge the feasibility of the tactical use of atomic weapons. On 5 July 1951, in the interval between the agreement to start peace talks and their actual opening, the Army Operations Division produced a memorandum recommending the use of the bomb if there was a deadlock in the talks. In the meantime it recommended field tests. Korea was the obvious place for these.

In September and October 1951, while the peace talks were suspended over violations of the neutral zone and during the fiercest land

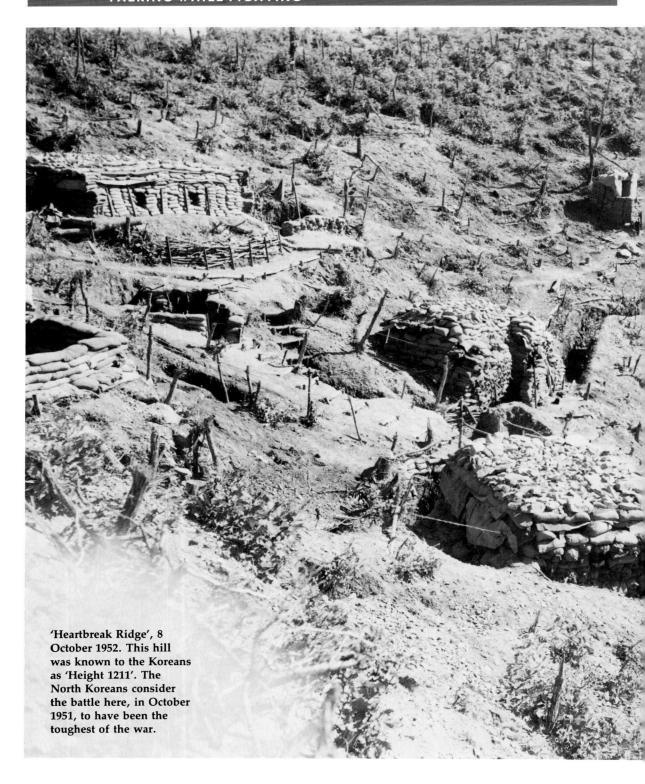

'Heartbreak Ridge', 8 October 1952. This hill was known to the Koreans as 'Height 1211'. The North Koreans consider the battle here, in October 1951, to have been the toughest of the war.

battle of the war between US and North Korean troops, on Height 1211/ Heartbreak Ridge, the USA carried out 'Operation Hudson Harbor' in conditions of utmost secrecy. Lone B–29 bombers flew over North Korea on simulated atomic-bombing runs, dropping dummy atomic bombs or heavy TNT bombs. The project called for 'actual functioning of all activities which would be involved in an atomic strike, including weapons assembly and testing, leading, ground control of bomb aiming' and the like. Although the project indicated that the bombs were probably not useful (for purely tactical reasons), one may imagine the steel nerves required of leaders in Pyongyang, observing on radar a lone B–29 simulating the attack lines that had resulted in the devastation of Hiroshima and Nagasaki just six years earlier, each time unsure whether the bomb was real or a dummy.

Additional pressure was put on the communist camp with the signing, in early September 1951, of the West's peace treaty with Japan in San Francisco.

Japan played a central role in the Korean war. It was a giant rear base for the USA – America's 'sanctuary'. It was the headquarters for MacArthur, Ridgway and Clark and was dotted with crucial US bases and airfields.

The Sino-Soviet treaty of February 1950 had identified Japan as the prime menace to peace in the Far East. Washington had encouraged the re-establishment of Japan's armed forces and had secretly deployed Japanese military forces in the Korean war. This was strenuously denied at the time by the US government – indeed, the charge was often singled out as a typical example of communist mendacity. The senior Japanese official in charge of Japan's minesweeping operation (technically a combat operation) in Korea in 1950, Admiral Takeo Okubo, spelled out to us the link between Japan's military role in the Korean war and the peace treaty: 'In effect, it was on the foundation laid by [the minesweepers'] achievement that the edifice of the peace treaty was erected. Up till then [the UN states] had not signed. In short, it was the achievements of this Special Minesweeping Flotilla, you might say, which made the peace treaty possible.'

To North Korea and China the Japanese peace treaty was not simply an innocuous document bringing what its name seemed to promise, peace, but also partly a restoration of war criminals who only some six years earlier had been carrying out acts of hideous cruelty against the inhabitants of Korea and China. The Chinese and North Koreans knew that the Americans had protected the top Japanese germ-warfare experts who had experimented on Chinese and Korean prisoners only a few years before.

Peace talks resumed at the new site of Panmunjom on 25 October 1951. By late November the two sides had tentatively agreed on a demarcation line. Chinese texts indicate that it was during the summer and early autumn of 1951 that the communist side began to feel confident of its ability to hold the line. The communists had built extensive underground fortifications, which they called 'an underground Great Wall', all along the front and in a horseshoe up the coast to both east and west. They dug a total

Peng Dehuai, *left*, at the front. When this picture was published recently in China the caption said that Peng often travelled to the front because he heard that many Chinese soldiers went blind because of malnutrition. The Chinese had a phrase – 'one handful of dried powder, the other hand a handful of snow' – to describe their predicament. Peng cancelled the rule that the troops had to finish any meal in five minutes flat because it was causing severe stomach problems.

of 776 miles of tunnels and 3,427 miles of trenches, involving the shifting of 78 million cubic yards of rock and earth. In these fortifications the armies could withstand even the most concentrated bombing from the US side.

From the middle of 1951 there was a huge expansion of the Chinese Air Force, which, by the latter stages of the war, had about 4,000 planes and had become the third largest air force in the world. US control of the skies, particularly from Pyongyang northwards, began to be challenged.

Little is known about how the Chinese and North Korean armies co-ordinated their actions. The Chinese mainly operated on the western side and the Koreans on the eastern front. On the whole they did not fight in combined units, but there was undoubtedly a joint command. The few outside observers who saw anything suggest that China, which supplied the majority of the troops, exercised ultimate authority. During the Cultural Revolution in China accusations were brought against Peng Dehuai that he had behaved in an authoritarian manner towards Kim Il Sung, but these accusations are unverified. The memoirs of Chinese Marshal Nie Rongzhen also suggest that China was critical of North Korean strategy, especially in the period that led up to the Chinese intervention.

Napalmed woman and child in North Korea.

Life in the North was dangerous and tough. A gruesome combination of instruments of destruction rained down. High explosives poured on to the towns and villages. Napalm was, in Churchill's phrase, 'splashed' over houses, farms, people, animals and stores. The official US military histories often describe the bombing from the air. But it was another matter to be on the ground. The mood of the time was grim. John Ford's 1951 film, *This is Korea!*, has appalling footage of napalm, no less horrifying for having been staged in part. Over one scene with a flame-thrower the commentary (read by John Wayne) simply says: 'Burn 'em out, cook 'em, fry 'em.'

166

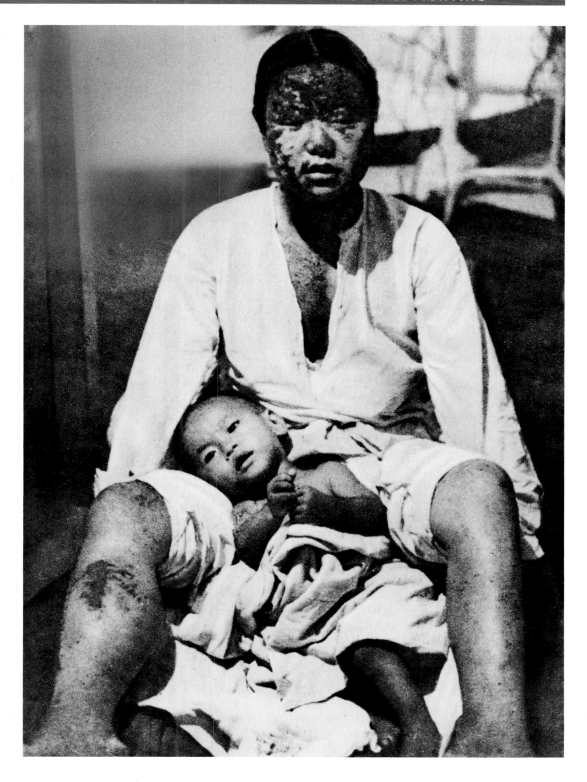

Dead children, North
Korea.

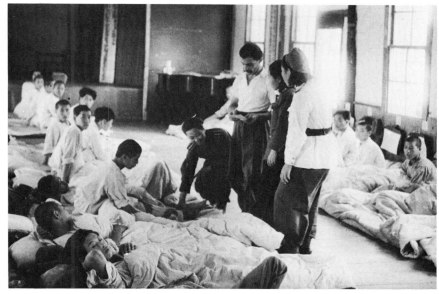

A hospital in North Korea, 1951. The Eastern European countries sent many doctors and nurses to work in North Korean hospitals.

Women working in a field in North Korea, 1951. Farming, like everything else, was under constant attack from the air, and much of it was carried on at night.

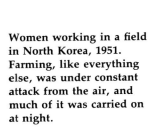

169

◁ North Korea's leader, Kim
Il Sung, in 1951.

Kim Il Sung's bunker
underneath Pyongyang, as
it is now presented.

Underground factory in
North Korea, 19 November
1950.

Air pressure was the single most important instrument for influencing the course of the war – and the peace talks, starting with escalating raids on Pyongyang in July and August 1951 as the talks got under way. The population of the city was now down to about 50,000 from half a million before the war. On 15 August 1951 the USA initiated 'Operation Strangle', a giant bombing campaign designed to cut communications routes and supply lines, described in the official US history of the Navy in Korea:

> In effect, the task of air power . . . was to sever the Korean peninsula at the Yalu and Tumen rivers, to undercut the peninsula, and to float the entire landmass out into mid-ocean where interdiction, in concert with a naval blockade, could strangle the supply lines of the communists and thereby force their retreat and defeat.

Most of the population left the bigger cities. Many children were sent abroad, some to China, others to Eastern Europe. Some women also were evacuated to China. Most of the population was reduced to what the British lawyer Jack Gaster, who visited the North in early 1952, told us was 'a troglodyte existence', living in caves and holes in the ground. The government operated from bunkers deep below ground. Tibor Meray has vividly described the scene in a government bunker in Pyongyang during a celebration for Liberation Day, 15 August 1952, emerging at dawn to see the streets lined with rows of corpses from the night's bombing. He, like others, wondered why anyone stayed in Pyongyang at all. Yet the speed and skill with which bridges and communications – and, later, dams – were repaired was described by US officials as 'phenomenal'. Almost all repair work had to be done at night, and casualties from delayed-action bombs were high. Intense efforts were made to exhaust the population by relentless bombing. One campaign was actually called 'Operation Insomnia'. The bombing also took a heavy toll on the Chinese troops. One Chinese soldier told us that by the time he was wounded (for the third time) towards the end of the war, he was the only man left in his unit (which had originally had 128 men) who had not been either killed or badly wounded.

By 1952 just about everything in North and central Korea was completely levelled. American officials sought to use aerial bombing as a type of psychological and social warfare. As Robert Lovett once put it, 'If we keep on tearing the place apart, we can make it a most unpopular affair for the North Koreans. We ought to go right ahead.'

Of course, the bombing was 'unpopular', but it did not break the people's morale. It is impossible to say how it affected the population's attitude to the regime of Kim Il Sung. Resistance to an external force can have a powerful cohesive effect, regardless of the nature of the government. The low point in the regime's popularity seems to have come not as a result of the bombing but in the period immediately after it re-occupied the North at the end of 1950 and engaged in reprisal killings and purges. What is perhaps most remarkable was the government's ability to function at all.

**Cartoon from the Chinese magazine *Manhua*, September 1951, depicting America's policy as two-faced ('Talking is false: the real intention is to promote Japan and invade Asia'). On the right, under a map of Korea, the sign says, 'Korean Ceasefire Negotiations', while Truman and Ridgway (arm in sling) stagger off. On the left Acheson is standing behind a Japanese militarist (*seated, with samurai sword*), who is holding a scroll that says, 'Plan to invade Asia'. The document on the table says, 'Japanese Peace Treaty Made in America'.**

Bringing the war home: a
British schoolboy and a
corporal at a display of
captured Soviet
equipment, Horse Guards
Parade, London, August
1951.

The Western press gave little idea of what life was like under American bombing. A comic shows an American soldier undergoing a crisis after only one raid – by his own side.

### The POW Issue Stalls the Peace Talks

During the 'second round' of talks, which lasted almost one year – from 25 October 1951 to 8 October 1952 – the repatriation of prisoners of war (POWs) emerged as the major issue.

The 1949 Geneva Convention on prisoners of war states: 'Prisoners of war shall be released and repatriated without delay after the cessation of hostilities' (Article 118). The USA had signed, *but not ratified*, this Convention. Neither China nor North Korea had signed the Convention. Both sides stated that they would adhere to its spirit. The communist side proposed that all POWs be repatriated immediately the armistice was signed. The US came up with a proposal that they called 'voluntary (or non-forcible) repatriation'. The communists argued that this contravened the Geneva Convention.

Internal US documents support this position. In the week

before talks opened in July 1951 a Joint Chiefs of Staff committee concluded that 'voluntary repatriation was attractive because it was humanitarian and aided psychological warfare, but dangerous because it violated the Geneva Convention and created a precedent that might injure America.' Acheson, who was a lawyer, agreed – in private. But he and Truman soon became key supporters of it, while Ridgway and other military figures strongly opposed it.

The stated aim of the proposal was to provide POWs with freedom of choice. The West argued that some prisoners did not want to go back where they came from and would be in danger if they were repatriated. They referred to Russian prisoners who were handed back at the end of World War II and were either executed or sent to the Gulag. The communist side said that violence was being exercised to prevent POWs from expressing their options in a free atmosphere.

The POW issue, as it affected the talks, hinged overwhelmingly on the question of how POWs in UN custody were being treated and

**Women and children in a South Korean prison camp at Kanaru, 15 January 1952.**

175

A group of Western POWs in a camp in North Korea. Most Western prisoners were held by the Chinese from 1951. Many photographs of Western POWs show them grinning and looking a bit too happy. This shot, taken by Polish journalist Lucjan Pracki, is one of the rare shots that show them as they probably felt a lot of the time – surly and not pleased at being paraded for photographers from the communist press.

whether they were able to exercise freedom of choice. As early as 17 February 1951 North Korea denounced the USA for 'slaughtering the Korean people and [Chinese] POWs'. The first prisoner rebellion took place in June 1951, on the island of Koje, mainly against poor food. Ridgway's headquarters revealed that by the end of 1951 6,600 POWs had died in UN custody. The announcement stated that the 6,600 deaths resulted *primarily* (authors' emphasis) from the poor physical condition of the prisoners when they arrived at UN camps. Many deaths were from starvation; others were due to lack of medical treatment; many were the result of violence. And it is the question of violence that lies at the core of the whole issue.

The way in which the camps were administered played a significant role. The USA assigned most of the guard duty to South Koreans, while encouraging anti-communist prisoners and agents to hold positions of power. The USA also brought in Nationalist personnel from Taiwan and allowed these to operate in positions of authority.

Violence was exercised by many different groups. Eventually, there developed a cycle of violence and reprisals, followed by counter-violence and counter-reprisals. The worst early violence was perpetrated by South Korean guards. According to Western sources, the guards often just killed prisoners. Many POWs died even before they got to the camps. Inside the camps pro- and anti-communist POWs soon began fighting over many issues, including food, as well as whether or not to be repatriated.

Documentation on violence among prisoners is scrappy, but a top-secret report from US Ambassador Muccio in July 1952 is probably close to the truth; it names 'both pro- and anti-Commie leaders Korean compounds, anti-commie leaders Chi[nese] compounds' as responsible for a long history of 'extreme coercion and intimidation'. Muccio does not mention pro-communist Chinese leaders. They too exercised pressure on POWs to return to the mainland, but the general consensus is that of the four groups of prisoners they were the least violent. Ample evidence exists of extreme violence by the three groups named by Muccio. British troops who went into Koje in summer 1952 found bodies of people who had been killed by pro-North Korean prisoners as waverers. Some had been drowned, others hauled up to the top of tents and tied up by their testicles, others speared. Similar violence occurred at the hands of anti-communist Korean POWs. Anti-communist Chinese killed men who wanted to return to the mainland, in one case by putting a fire hose up a man's anus. They cut hunks of flesh out of men's arms and paraded waverers in front of basins containing the flesh and the hearts of pro-mainland POWs who had been murdered, telling the waverers that was what would happen to them if they did not opt for Taiwan.

**Captured guerrillas, Chonju, 14 January 1952, during 'Operation Ratkiller', the big anti-guerrilla drive in the South.**

It was on 18 February 1952 that the USA first formally suggested not returning all POWs. From this point on there were major revolts among prisoners against pressure on them not to return home. For a period there was, in theory, a process termed 'screening' that, it was claimed, would allow a prisoner to opt for or against repatriation. In fact, it did not

work out that way, and 'screening' often meant intimidation and torture. Many POWs were forcibly tattooed with anti-communist slogans to make it more difficult for them to choose to return home. US documents of the time show that there was what one State Department official called a 'reign of terror' in the camps – and that senior US officials knew this. US Ambassador Muccio later called the guards 'Gestapos'.

According to the USA's first chief negotiator at the peace talks, Admiral Joy, anyone who expressed a wish to return home was 'either beaten black and blue *or killed* [authors' emphasis] . . . the majority of the POWs were too terrified to frankly express their choice.' Joy wrote this in his diary. In public he gave quite a different impression.

Violence was not the exclusive prerogative of the Koreans and Chinese. When the pro-communist POWs revolted during 1952 the USA instituted a 'shoot-to-kill' policy. Ridgway moved a battalion of tanks 200

The caption on the AP photo reads: 'Wounded Red prisoners, some aided by companions, are herded out of Koje Island POW camp's compound 76 after bloody fight with US paratroopers, 10 June [1952]. Thirty-one were killed and eighty-five wounded. US officers are directing roundup from tower in background.'

miles from the front line, to Koje. In his own words, he ordered Van Fleet 'to use whatever force was necessary . . . I was determined that if the Red POWs made any resistance, or attempted any delay in carrying out our demands, we would shoot, and I wanted the killing machinery on hand to do a thorough job of it.' Van Fleet told his officers: 'I will be much more critical of your using less force than necessary than too much.' UN troops later went in with tanks and flame-throwers and killed hundreds of POWs in different incidents.

On 8 May 1952 the prisoners on Koje seized the American camp commandant, Brigadier-General Francis T. Dodd, and held him for three days until his replacement, Brigadier-General Charles F. Colson, signed a statement acknowledging forced 'screening' and that 'Many prisoners of war have been killed and wounded by UN forces.' The USA then repudiated the statement.

In May 1952 the Americans called in British and Canadian forces to help put down the revolts on Koje. The main motive seems to have been to involve two key allies in the operation. Canada's participation set off a political storm at home, and the government had to sacrifice the senior officer on the spot. British participation did not provoke as much furore – largely because the truth was concealed at the time.

No one knows how many POWs would have liked to return, or to stay, given a genuinely free choice. Given that some 70 per cent of the Chinese soldiers had recently been in the Nationalist armies, it is impossible to say whether their allegiance to Chiang Kai-shek was stronger than their hopes for life under the communists. Two translators working for the USA told Joy that an honest 'screening' in the Nationalist-dominated compounds would find 85 per cent, not the recorded 15 per cent, opting for repatriation. Given that the Nationalist-dominated compounds made up well over half the total, if extrapolated, this would give a figure of over 90 per cent of Chinese POWs wishing to return to the People's Republic of China. One crucial question was 'Do you want to go to "Free China"?' The Nationalists meant Taiwan. Many POWs thought they meant the People's Republic and replied, 'Yes.' Internal US documents show that a large number of POWs were not able to express their wishes freely.

The UN side said the communists were maltreating Western prisoners. On 14 November 1951 the Judge-Advocate of the US 8th Army, Colonel James Hanley, issued a statement claiming that over 5,500 US prisoners had been 'massacred' since the war began. Only much later was it explained that there was evidence that a much lower number – 365 US POWs – had died as the result of 'atrocities'. The rest was a 'presumption' – based, as it turned out, on mythical figures. There is no consensus on the UN side either about the figures or about what actually happened. British documents show that the British government did not accept the US view and regarded most of the American evidence as unconvincing and some of it as misleading.

The second main US complaint came later on, as some

prisoners began to make statements and confessions. The USA claimed that the communists were 'brainwashing' POWs to persuade them to denounce their own governments, engage in peace campaigns, confess to war crimes and decide against repatriation.

Most of the deaths among UN captives occurred in the first winter of the war. Some of these deaths came while the prisoners were being marched north. One US officer, Lieutenant Thornton, was shot by a North Korean officer, 'the Tiger', in front of other POWs. Other US prisoners who collapsed were apparently shot. An internal British document noted that not one British soldier on this 'Death March' died. No Turks died in captivity. Conditions varied from camp to camp, often greatly. There were cases of prolonged and inhumane interrogation—in some cases even after the armistice was signed.

In the camps approximately 2,700 American prisoners died. Some of these deaths were the result of lack of medical facilities and disease following on malnutrition. Some soldiers froze to death. Some died from beatings by guards. Quite a number of prisoners died from what was called 'give-up-itis'. Two other causes less often mentioned were US bombing and murder at the hands of fellow prisoners (after the war some POWs were tried and sentenced in the USA for this). Prisoners were often lodged in ordinary villages (the Koreans had no camps prepared). The Koreans did not identify these sites.

Two images dominate Western accounts: brutal North Koreans, and Chinese 'brainwashing'. Korean civilians often attacked Western POWs, particularly *en route* to detention centres, but equally Korean guards sometimes protected Western prisoners from locals. In other cases they killed Western prisoners. But North Koreans also released some captives early on, and these reported good treatment by their captors.

During 1951 the Chinese took over custody of almost all the Western prisoners; it seems the main reason was that they felt that Korean treatment of the POWs made the communist side vulnerable. Western POWs have told us of Chinese guards protecting them from irate Korean civilians. One Chinese officer told us that when Chinese were escorting Western prisoners to the rear they were ordered never to leave them in case the Koreans got at them. Many Western POWs reported that Chinese medical personnel and field hospitals made remarkable efforts for prisoners in very difficult circumstances.

Another aspect of the issue was the use of violence, intimidation and subtler pressures, particularly on US airmen to elicit confessions about germ warfare. In many cases the Chinese tried to get POWs to make statements about misdeeds that were verifiable, such as the bombing of civilian targets. But these documents were the product of a political culture that put confession before truth. The Chinese often re-wrote and 'edited' statements, framing them in stilted denunciations of Wall Street and other bogeys. The statements – or parts of them (which was enough) – looked implausible to Western eyes, and the framing allowed Western governments convincingly to discredit entire documents that often contained considerable truth.

Most POWs, though often cold and hungry, were not subjected to intolerable or brutal pressures. Many British POWs reported decent treatment, given the general conditions. Pressure was not applied to prevent prisoners from returning to their homes. The sole British POW who chose to remain with the communists, Andrew Condron, told us that the Chinese tried hard to persuade him and more than twenty Americans declining repatriation to return home.

At first the communists refused to confront the question of how many POWs wanted to go where, but in the end they accepted the principle of choice. Having done so, they said that the choice must be really free. The USA dug in on non-forcible repatriation, while allowing free choice to be violated in the camps for which it was responsible.

The two sides disagreed about supervision. The USA tried, until near the very end, to make the UN the umpire. The communists tried to get the USSR accepted as a 'neutral' member of the commission supervising the implementation of POWs' choice but then dropped the proposal in favour of a balanced commission of non-belligerents.

Some prisoners of war were badly treated by both sides. But the UN side was responsible for more deaths and, as far as can be verified, more violence than the communists – among more prisoners, of course. This unpalatable truth, which was vigorously concealed at the time, was clearly spelt out recently by Britain's former Chief of the Defence Staff, Field Marshal Lord Carver: 'The UN prisoners in Chinese hands, although subject to "re-education" processes of varying intensity . . . were certainly much better off in every way than any held by the Americans, whether the latter's compounds were dominated by the communists or by the Korean or Chinese nationalists.' The violence by the two custodian sides was also exercised for different ends: only the UN side applied violence to prevent repatriation.

On the US side the main concern appears to have been to inflict a propaganda defeat on the communists – and, in particular, on the Chinese. The POW issue can be seen as the second side of a larger propaganda battle, whose goal was to try to show that a majority of people opposed communism and, by implication, supported anti-communism (personified by Syngman Rhee for Korea and Chiang Kai-shek for China). This result had not been demonstrated either in the civil struggles in the two countries or in the separate elections in South Korea. The only two sizeable groups available to try to make the point were refugees and POWs. What these two groups had in common was that they were extremely vulnerable and, although un-free, could speak, or be persuaded to speak, with a semblance of freedom. The USA went purposefully after Chinese POWs, as they had greater propaganda value.

It was perfectly fair of the West to express concern about how a communist state might treat political undesirables or unknowns. There are

no guarantees in such cases. The communist camp and its supporters brushed off this point. The US position was also hypocritical, however: the principle of 'voluntary repatriation' covered both the attempt to enable genuine anti-communists to avoid enforced repatriation and a forcible, often brutal, campaign to compel large numbers of POWs to refuse repatriation.

In the middle of the Koje upheaval Ridgway was replaced as Commander of the US/UN forces by General Mark Clark (a change planned earlier). The USA also removed its chief negotiator at Panmunjom, Admiral Joy, who had been put in a difficult position by the Koje events. He was replaced on 22 May by US Army Lieutenant-General William K. Harrison.

**FM Lord Alexander (British Defence Minister), Paek Sun-yop (ROKA) and James Van Fleet (USA), 16 June 1952. Alexander went to Korea to assess the aftermath of the POW rebellions on Koje, where British troops had been deployed against prisoners.**

### Complications: the Germ Warfare Question

Meanwhile a new element had been introduced into the negotiations: the accusation that the USA had used germ warfare. In February–March 1952 North Korea and China charged that the USA had dropped a large number of diseases from the air, including plague, anthrax, cholera and encephalitis. Vectors named included flies, fleas, spiders, clams and feathers. The accusations also named animal and plant diseases. Shortly thereafter the Chinese began to release statements by captured US personnel confessing to having engaged in germ warfare.

The Western governments denied the charges *in toto*. Both sides called for an investigation but could not agree on who should carry it out. The West rejected confessions as admissible evidence, as they had been obtained under conditions in which the signatories were not free. The Western rebuttal was strengthened by the fact that there were many manifest signs of Chinese 'editing' of statements. The confessions were exactly that – confessions.

When the POWs were released in 1953 the ones who had confessed to germ warfare were put under strict control. Shortly thereafter the US government presented recantations signed by about one-quarter of those who had confessed. These recantations are generally accepted as valid by the West. The plain fact of the matter is that, while the confessions – and the recantations – have to be taken into account and evaluated, the issue cannot be decided either way on this basis.

The French writer Claude Roy visited North Korea in June 1952; he met the first two American airmen who had signed confessions, Quinn and Enoch. Roy told us that Quinn spoke in stilted jargon and stood by his confession. Enoch got Roy on his own and told him that his confession was a load of rubbish and that he had signed it only to make sure he got home.

**A cartoon from the Soviet satirical magazine *Krokodil*, depicting US Secretary of State Dean Acheson as a bug. The germ-warfare campaign became a big issue in the communist camp in 1952.**

The most extensive investigation of the issue on the spot, in north-east China and Korea, was one carried out in July–August 1952 by a group of radical scientists, all except one from Western countries. This commission contained eminent people with the requisite scientific skills, including parasitologists and microbiologists. Among them was Joseph Needham, who as British scientific attaché in China during World War II had witnessed Japanese germ warfare and spoke fluent Chinese, so could question witnesses directly. The commission published a 665-page report, which concluded that the charges were true.

The conclusions are based mainly on two elements: work reported by Chinese and North Korean scientists in the period before the commission arrived, and detailed examination and analysis of medical evidence by the commission. The commission did not witness any case of germ warfare at first hand.

The Western governments, while dismissing the charges as baseless, did not produce a detailed scientific refutation of the evidence. The two main components of the West's case were that the diseases could have happened naturally, given war, malnutrition and lack of medical facilities, and that the USA would not have engaged in something that was universally recognized to be a war crime.

There is some doubt about whether all the diseases named could have happened naturally, especially one called haemorrhagic fever, as the Japanese bacteriologist Professor Tsuneishi detailed. Some other parts of the generally accepted Western refutations can be shown to be unfounded – for example, the claim that the delivery systems suggested were ridiculous (very similar ones had, in fact, been used by the Japanese in World War II).

The argument that probably carried most weight was that the USA could not have used a weapon as horrible as germ warfare, though nothing can be established by this assertion. The USA was engaged in germ-warfare research. It had employed Japanese and Nazi germ-warfare experts and was at the time rushing through work on the nerve gas Sarin, a chemical weapon that was banned by the Geneva Convention. The evidence shows preparations for using germ warfare (which do not prove anything about whether it was used or not).

The USA lied about its re-employment of Japanese germ-warfare experts (who had committed verified war crimes), and this under-

Hungarian journalist Tibor ▷ Meray examining flies in North Korea, early 1952. Meray was taken there by North Korean officials, who told him that the flies had been dropped by American planes and were infected. In 1957, after leaving Hungary, Meray submitted the Korean evidence to scientists in France, who concluded that it did not stand up.

◁

Soviet correspondent Vitali S. Latov with a bomb casing, North Korea, 1952. Latov, whom we interviewed, described this as a germ bomb and said that he and other people had fallen ill with 'Japanese tropical fever' shortly after it dropped.

The International Scientific Commission (ISC) on Germ Warfare with Chinese leaders, Beijing, summer 1952. *From the left:* Guo Moruo, Zhou Enlai, Qian Sanqiang, Joseph Needham (UK), Mao Zedong, Zhukov-Verezhnikov (USSR), Kowalski (USSR), Andreen (Sweden), Olivo (Italy), Mme Pessoa (Brazil), Graziosi (Italy), Pessoa (Brazil), Malterre (France), unidentified. Mao greeted the delegates with two sallies: 'Don't make too much of all this! They've tried using biochemical warfare, but it hasn't been too successful'; and 'What are all these uninfected insects they are dropping?' The left-wing ISC investigated charges of germ warfare in North Korea and north-east China.

mines – though it does not invalidate – other denials. One cannot dismiss the accusations simply by claiming that the West must be telling the truth.

If one is to believe the Western case, it is also necessary to take it through to its logical conclusion, which is that the North Koreans and the Chinese mounted a spectacular piece of fraudulent theatre, involving the mobilization of thousands (probably tens of thousands) of people in China and Korea; getting scores of top Chinese doctors and scientists and myriad lesser personnel, as well as Zhou Enlai and other senior Chinese figures, to fake evidence, lie and invent at least one extremely *recherché* medical fraud. Needham himself acknowledged at the time that 'a patriotic conspiracy' – that is, a gigantic fraud – was a possibility. Some of the filmed evidence that the Chinese presented does not stand up.

Tibor Meray (who now lives in the West) has confirmed that he saw flies in temperatures far below zero degrees Centigrade. Not only were the flies alive (raising the question of whether they had been especially bred), but they were reproducing. Two questions arise from this: who put the flies there? And were they infected? At the time Meray reported that the Americans dropped them from planes and that they were infected. In 1957, after reaching the West, he consulted eminent scientists in France and wrote that the evidence on which he had based his earlier statements was scientifically unsound. He has said that he thinks the flies were most probably placed there by the Chinese, not the Koreans, leaving open the question of whether the flies were infected or not.

As the evidence stands, the issue is open. There are strong and weak points in the case on each side and many unexplained points. One must also entertain the possibility that *both* sides are lying in part. The communist camp was eminently capable both of faking evidence and of exaggerating evidence even when it was perfectly strong. It can be proved that parts of the US military were prepared to envisage violating the Geneva

Convention. It is possible that the USA used certain weapons on an experimental basis and that the Chinese blew its actions up into a 'mass-extermination' campaign. A 'middle-way' hypothesis is also possible: that the USA dropped uninfected insects to test how they survived.

Although most people in the West believed their governments' denials, the accusations had two effects: they made people in the USA wonder about the ability of their personnel to stand up to pressure in captivity and led to widespread concern about 'brainwashing'; and they sowed seeds of doubt world-wide. When Ridgway arrived in Europe to take up his post as head of NATO a few weeks later there were gigantic demonstrations against him, which rocked the French government. The walls of Paris were covered with slogans saying 'Ridgway, Go Home!' and graffiti denouncing him for germ warfare.

The airmen's confessions about germ warfare were followed within days by official acknowledgement that violence had been used on POWs in UN custody. With two sets of confessions within the space of one month, the communists had staked out a new position both in the world at large and at Panmunjom. Many in the West now had come to see the war as a 'dirty' one. Their ally, Syngman Rhee, did little to dispel this view.

**Street inoculation, Pyongyang, 1952.**

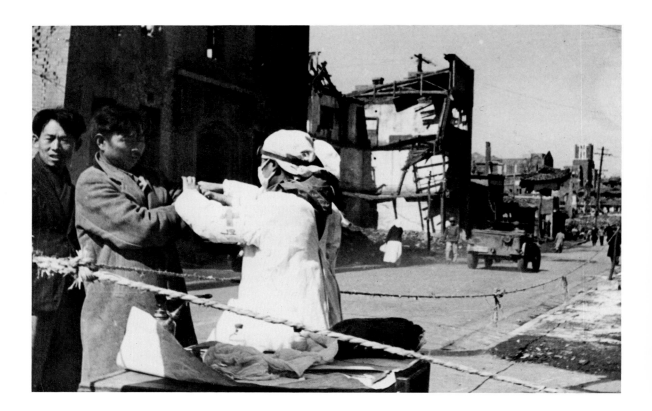

Syngman Rhee with General Van Fleet and General Yi Chong-chan, Kwangju, January 1952. Yi was commander of the first ROK forces to cross the parallel on 1 October 1950.

### Clark Ups the Stakes

On 17 February 1952 agreement was reached on holding a political conference within three months after an armistice to discuss the withdrawal of foreign troops and the peaceful settlement (that is, the re-unification) of Korea. Rhee did not like the sound of this. He moved to crush his surviving domestic political opponents through trials and intimidation. He also moved to set up his own army, independent of UN/US control. On 25 May he declared martial law. Control of the military became a key mechanism for fund-raising, which meant, broadly, the looting of military supplies and foodstuffs. Army pay at the time was the dollar equivalent of 50 cents a month, while captains got the equivalent of $6.

It was now that the USA began seriously to discuss getting rid of Rhee. When General Mark Clark took over from Ridgway in May 1952 he proposed 'Operation Everready', the code-name for a plan to oust – and possibly arrest – Rhee.

He also conducted a general review of military options and suggested the consideration of a number of steps, including use of the atomic bomb, 'unleashing' Chiang Kai-shek and increasing air pressure on the North.

On 23 June American planes bombed the four most vital dams and power complexes in North Korea for the first time. One of these was the huge Supung dam on the Yalu. The dam supplied about 90 per cent of North Korea's total power, and about 10 per cent of the power of north-east China. The raid on Supung was the biggest single strike of the Korean war and involved more than 500 US planes. It blasted the generator plant on the Korean side. There was a blackout all over North Korea for two weeks; the

North was deprived of almost all its electrical power for the rest of the war. At the same time, and more covertly, the USA attacked a whole series of factories and mines, including further heavy raids on the monazite mines that supplied a key mineral for the Soviet atomic bomb.

**Pyongyang being bombed by B-29s.**

The bombing of Supung strained relations between the USA and its allies, especially Britain. The USA was supposed to consult Britain before it took such a step. Presumably deliberately, it did not. In the House of Commons Foreign Secretary Eden openly pleaded for 'no more surprises'.

Beginning on 11 and 12 July, US bombers, along with Australian, South African and South Korean planes, carried out a series of huge raids on Pyongyang. The North Koreans reported 2,000 dead and 4,000 wounded from these first sorties – including over a hundred casualties among UN POWs. A top-level Chinese delegation headed by Zhou Enlai was visiting Moscow, and the USA wanted the bombing to 'send a signal' to the participants. The bombing of Pyongyang escalated to a massive raid on 29 August, the war's heaviest attack on the city. North Korea reported 6,000 civilian deaths (out of a population of less than 50,000) from this one raid alone. According to the London *Times*, fifteen minutes' warning was given

188

**Pyongyang after US bombing.**

of the raid – enough time for anyone trying to flee to be caught out in the open. Altogether 1,403 sorties were flown in this raid; the official communiqué said that 10,000 litres of napalm were dropped 'with excellent results'; 62,000 rounds of ammunition were employed in 'strafing at low level'; 697 tons of bombs were dropped. In the middle of this campaign the USA announced that it was warning civilians 'to stay away from military targets in seventy-eight Korean cities, towns and villages that have been converted into military centres'.

In early autumn the communists launched their biggest attack of the year in the central sector north-west of Chorwon. The USA replied with its biggest offensive for a year north of Kumhwa, at Sangkumryung/ Triangle Ridge. The Chinese regard this as the most critical, and the most terrible, battle of the war. The day after this battle was joined the USA staged a large-scale amphibious landing operation in the direction of Wonsan, which seemed as though it might be a second 'Inchon'. According to Marshal Nie, the intelligence reports went right up to Mao, who agreed with the recommendation that the US move was a feint. The peace talks were broken off.

Once again, the guns had taken over from the truce tent.

189

# ARMISTICE WITHOUT REUNIFICATION

Opposition to the war was mounting: in Britain, with Churchill increasingly disaffected and hostile to Rhee; in the still inchoate Third World, where many important states, like Argentina, Egypt and Chile, had refused to send troops to back the USA; and in the USA itself. Eisenhower campaigned as the Republican candidate for the US presidency on the pledge 'I shall go to Korea.' This was widely interpreted to mean that he would try to end the war. It is generally accepted that this pledge was central to his election to the presidency.

On 20 January 1953 Eisenhower was inaugurated as President of the USA. On 2 February his State of the Union address threatened a significant expansion of the war. He announced that he had instructed that the 7th Fleet should be 'no longer employed to shield communist China'. In other words, Chiang Kai-shek was to be 'unleashed'.

What he was doing was not winding down the war, but switching the focus to China from Korea, where there was almost nothing left to destroy and about which Stalin probably cared little. In Korea, Van Fleet was replaced on 11 February 1953 by General Maxwell Taylor, who was less given to risking high US casualties – the key factor in establishing American attitudes. This helped to tranquillize public opinion at home. Eisenhower had already endeared himself to the US public by launching the slogan 'Let it be Asians against Asians' during the presidential election campaign.

Eisenhower was helped by the fact that he took office in the middle of winter. Fighting in Korea was in a state of relative lull, partly because neither side thought it could make much headway in the bitter cold. There was thus a breathing space, during which each side took the measure of the other. The communists had nearly 1 million troops facing some 800,000 on the UN side as the New Year came in.

Most well-informed sources suggest that Eisenhower threatened China directly with atomic bombs. On 24 February China sent a top-level delegation to Moscow, headed by the nation's leading atomic physicist, Qian Sanqiang. It is believed that Qian went to ask Stalin for either the means of retaliation or a nuclear guarantee if Eisenhower used the bomb against China.

On 5 March Stalin died. Events now moved fast. On 15 March

**Trying to stay alive: a South Korean woman and stall.**

Gen. Maxwell Taylor, new commander of the 8th Army, with his predecessor Van Fleet, *left*, Syngman Rhee and General Mark Clark, 11 February 1953. Taylor drew important strategic lessons from Korea, which he formulated in his influential book *The Uncertain Trumpet*; these ideas greatly influenced John Kennedy and led directly to the US involvement in Vietnam, where Taylor worked as US Ambassador.

Eisenhower at Chorwon, 4 December 1952, with ROK Chief of Staff General Chong Il-gwon, *left*, during his secret visit to Korea.

Stalin's designated successor, Malenkov, said, 'There is no disputed or unresolved question that cannot be settled peacefully . . .'

The first thing the new group did after Stalin's funeral was to bring back the veteran Molotov, who had been out of power during the Korean war. Immediately after high-level Sino-Soviet discussions at Stalin's funeral, the Sino-North Korean side announced its acceptance of a proposal to discuss the exchange of sick and wounded prisoners. It seems that a decision was taken by the new Soviet leadership, especially Molotov, to try to bring the war to an end.

The communist acceptance of the proposal to exchange sick and wounded POWs also explicitly suggested that this could lead to a definitive settlement. The exchange of sick and wounded ('Little Switch') started on 20 April.

In early April the British and French civilians who had been captured after Seoul fell in June 1950 had suddenly been freed. Among these was George Blake, who had been head of British intelligence in Seoul before the war and who was later accused of being a Soviet agent, was jailed for forty-two years and then escaped to the USSR. The prevailing official British view is that he was 'turned' by the Russians while in captivity in Korea. Blake himself, in the only interview he gave after he got to the USSR, implied that he had been affected by revulsion at what the Americans did in Korea. The French journalist Maurice Chanteloup, who was in captivity with Blake, told us that Blake was very anti-American right from

A napalmed North Korean POW being repatriated at Panmunjom, 1953.

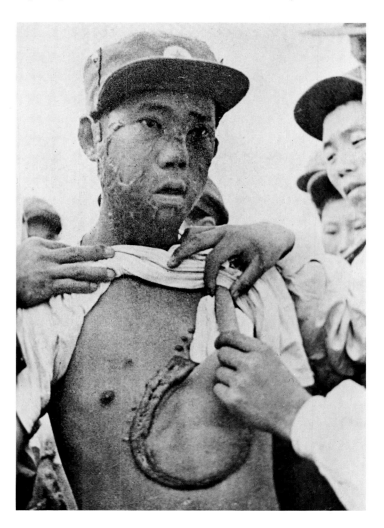

*Nightmare of War and Dream of Peace* by the left-wing Mexican painter Diego Rivera. This painting, which was commissioned by the Mexican government, was immediately cut down after diplomatic pressure. It had two main themes: the collection of signatures for the Stockholm Peace Appeal, and the atrocities in Korea, behind which hovers a huge atomic mushroom.

the beginning of the war. Both Chanteloup and the *Observer* correspondent Philip Deane, who was also imprisoned with Blake, have cast doubt on whether the Soviet interrogator who is alleged to have 'turned' Blake was really of the calibre to be entrusted with such a task. (The interrogator, who was a White Russian, himself later defected to the USA, where Deane unexpectedly bumped into him at a smart cocktail party in Washington.) Of course, Blake may already have been a Soviet agent.

### 'The Ultimate in Air Pressure': Bombing the Dams

The USA returned to full-dress talks on 26 April. Over the next few weeks the two sides reached agreement both that POWs who did not definitely want to return would be placed in some form of neutral custody and on the composition of a Neutral Nations Repatriation Commission to supervise the process.

Ground fighting started increasing again in the spring. Casualties rose steadily on both sides but with a markedly higher ratio of UN casualties to those on the communist side compared with earlier figures. In April 1953 the UN had nearly half as many front-line casualties as the communists – an unprecedentedly high proportion (4,343:10,500). UN casualties rose in May to 7,570, with the ratio about the same.

The USA simultaneously stepped up pressure on several fronts. It agreed to Rhee's request to expand his army by six divisions, bringing its total strength to twenty divisions.

It further escalated the air war both against China and inside

Korea. On 13 May the USA launched its first raids on a number of dams near Pyongyang. The main US Air Force study remarks: 'These strikes, largely passed over by the press, military observers, and news commentators . . . constituted one of the most significant air operations of the Korean war.' US General Weyland, Commander of the Far East and UN Air Forces, called these attacks 'perhaps the most spectacular [strike] of the war'.

The USA initially chose five dams near Pyongyang that supplied water for the irrigation system of the area that produced three-quarters of the country's rice. The US Air Force study comments: 'Attacks in May would be most effective psychologically' because it was the end of the rice-transplanting season before the roots become firmly embedded. The first strike, on 13 May, hit the Toksan dam above Pyongyang. 'The subsequent flash flood scooped clean 27 miles of valley below . . . Flood conditions extended as far downstream as Pyongyang, causing considerable damage to the capital city.' A similar attack on another dam, Chasan, on 15 and 16 May caused 'tremendous destruction of the rice crop . . . The flood water surging down the Taedong river inundated large parts of the North Korean capital city of Pyongyang.' The extent of the danger is shown by the fact that US intelligence was concerned that the flood waters might reach Seoul.

A message from British Prime Minister Churchill to US President Eisenhower. At that moment Rhee was endangering the signing of an armistice. Handwritten at the bottom are the words 'The Queen – by No. 10 [Downing Street, the official residence of the Prime Minister]'.

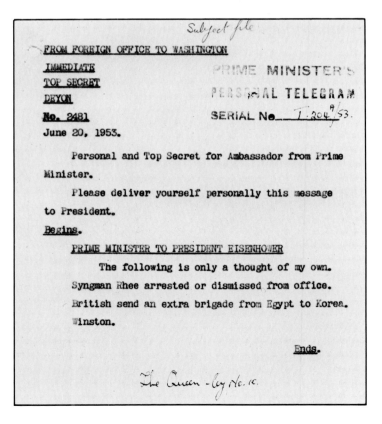

195

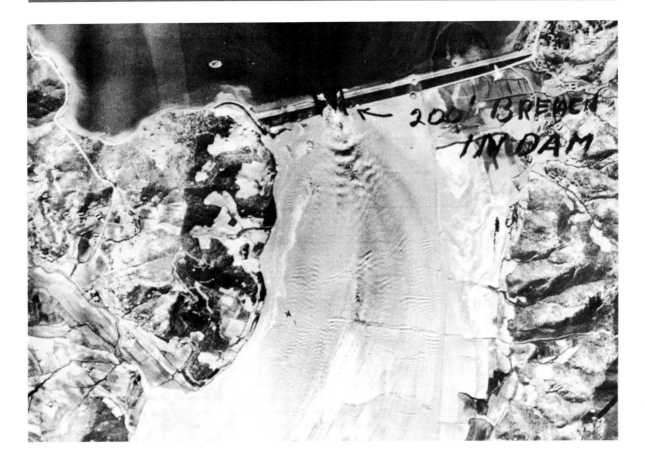

Almost *en passant*, the study notes that these floods would 'destroy the rat-holed supplies dispersed throughout the valleys and rural villages'. Hardly anyone commented on the fact that not only were supplies underground ('rat-holed') but also key military installations – and a large part of the civilian population. The same study comments: 'To the UN Command the breaking of the irrigation dams meant disruption of the enemy's lines of communication and supply. But to the communists the smashing of the dams meant primarily the destruction of their chief sustenance – rice. The Westerner can little conceive the awesome meaning that the loss of this staple food commodity has for the Asian – starvation and slow death.' The last time an act of this kind had been carried out, which was by the Nazis in Holland in 1944, it had been deemed a war crime at Nuremberg. The study remarks that the attacks on the dams produced 'the most vindictive, vitriolic propaganda indictments' of the Korean war.

Apart from the disruption and destruction of communications, lives and food, the bombing caused a huge diversion of manpower and energy into repairs. The Air Force study noted 'repair activity unequalled during the Korean War' at Toksan. It also noted that 'The work

The Chasan dam, North Korea, May 1953. In what the US Air Force commander called 'the ultimate in air pressure', in May 1953 the USA hit five dams north of Pyongyang, causing gigantic flooding, which reached as far as Pyongyang. The stated aim was to destroy the nation's rice crop, with widespread 'collateral damage', including the flooding of towns, villages, supplies, railways, bridges and roads – plus the drowning of untold numbers of people.

was carried out round-the-clock, with complete disregard to the delayed-action bombs strewn over the target area.' Another official US military history described this endeavour to repair vital facilities among delayed-action bombs as an example of 'oriental fatalism'.

These raids must have had a major impact. All previous attacks could, at high cost, somehow be contained. The only preventive action that the North Koreans could take was to drain the dams at the cost of depriving themselves of the water for their basic crop, rice.

### Armistice

In the middle of the bombing of the dams the talks were adjourned once again, on 16 May. In India Secretary of State Dulles told Premier Nehru, for onward transmission, that the USA was prepared to use the atomic bomb. Asked how he would feel if a peace agreement were reached at once, Dulles replied: 'We'd be worried. I don't think we can get much out of a Korean settlement until we have shown – before all Asia – our clear superiority by giving the Chinese one hell of a licking.'

But by now the momentum for peace was very strong. On 8 June a basic agreement was signed covering the POW question. Everyone seemed satisfied – except Syngman Rhee. He now decided to try to sabotage the agreement.

Rhee's plan was simple and effective: he would use the only weapon under his control – the POWs. On 17 June agreement was reached on the final truce-demarcation line. On the night of 18 June Rhee's officials organized a mass break-out of over 27,000 Korean POWs. To do so, South Koreans locked up US guards and knocked some unconscious, in one case by shoving their heads into water barrels. One South Korean officer told us that Korean guards shot and killed a number of US soldiers. The number two official involved has written that the Koreans were ordered to 'aim [their] rifles at the living quarters of American soldiers' and says that Americans opened fire in several cases, killing sixty-one escaping POWs. A former prisoner has said that about 300 POWs were killed in one camp alone.

According to Eisenhower's Chief of Staff, Sherman Adams, this was the only time that Eisenhower was ever woken during the night on government business during his presidency. In the House of Commons Churchill denounced Rhee for 'treachery' and in private advocated getting rid of him and possibly abandoning Korea completely. Eisenhower confided to his diary that if it were not for the strategic importance of Japan, he felt that most of the allies would have pulled out of Korea. The possibility of the disintegration of the Western alliance was a major factor in persuading the USA to sign the armistice.

Eisenhower and Dulles also dusted off 'Operation Everready'. Sherman Adams reports an intriguing exchange at this time:

Eisenhower told the Cabinet again, as he had often told them during the truce negotiations, that he wished the South Koreans would overthrow Rhee . . . Henry Cabot Lodge [US ambassador to the UN] mentioned that he had talked with General Mac-Arthur on an airliner a few days previously and the General had predicted that Rhee would be killed within a few weeks.

'On what basis?' Eisenhower asked.

'The General thinks that when this emotion dies down and the South Koreans have a chance for more reflection, certain elements will act,' Lodge said.

Eisenhower and Dulles told the Cabinet that Rhee was 'in a position to throw Korea and the entire Far East into chaotic bloodshed'. There is no sign that they thought Rhee was bluffing. The communists decided that the way to get Rhee's compliance was to hit his forces hard. On 24–25 June they launched a major offensive against part of the line held by the South Korean Army. In one week's fighting the South Koreans lost 7,400 men. The attack did not merely hit Koreans; it also endangered US troops. In June 1953 the UN fired the highest number of artillery shells of any month in the entire war. UN casualties soared to 23,161 for the month, compared with 36,346 on the communist side. Eisenhower told his Cabinet that 'a Red counter-attack would be likely to wipe out Rhee's forces and, along with them, the adjoining American and United Nations units in the remaining third of the front-line sector.' Eisenhower also knew that the war was increasingly unpopular with the troops: by 1952 desertions among US troops on the way to the front had increased by five times since the early months of the war. Many soldiers were invaliding themselves out of the war by inflicting wounds on themselves: according to internal British government documents, 90 per cent of those hospitalized were in for self-inflicted wounds.

The Sino-Korean side asked the USA whether it would ensure Rhee's compliance with the terms of the armistice. The USA hedged. The communists therefore launched another massive assault, on 13 July, again taking aim at South Korean troops. Communist casualties were very high in this week-long onslaught, but so were South Korean losses. According to Bacchus, 'The carnage in those two thrusts [June and July] was unprecedented.' The last three months of the war were in many ways the bitterest of all, with well over 2 million troops facing each other by July 1953, 1,200,000 on the communist side and 932,000 on the UN side. US sources estimate Chinese losses alone at over 72,000 in the one week of fighting in mid-July, with 25,000 killed. UN casualties came to 29,629. But the attack worked. The USA committed itself to taking responsibility for Rhee's compliance with the armistice. On 27 July 1953 an armistice was finally signed. The North Korean and Chinese commanders signed it on one side; the USA signed for the other side. South Korea did not sign the armistice – and to this day still has not.

It seems plausible to argue that each side found a way to hurt

UN Commander Gen. Mark Clark signing the armistice at base camp at Munsan-ni, 27 July 1953.

Kim Il Sung signing the armistice documents handed to him by chief negotiator Gen. Nam Il, 27 July 1953. In later years the North stopped showing pictures of Kim signing the armistice, as portrayal of the event moved increasingly towards depicting it as a 'US surrender'.

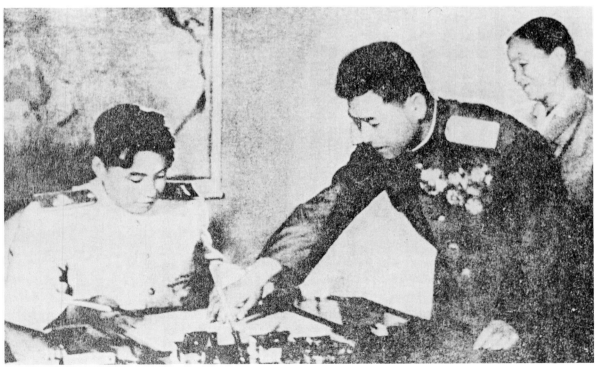

North Korean soldiers fraternizing with Americans the day after the armistice, 28 July 1953. There was considerable fraternization by the communist troops. Western reports often suggest, incorrectly, that this was only by Chinese. The US command tried, unsuccessfully, to ban fraternization.

the other enough to force a truce: the US bombing of the dams in May 1953 was a blow for which there was no effective counter-measure on the part of North Korea; the enormous casualties inflicted by the communists on the UN in June and July (combined with the West's disaffection with Rhee) made continuation of the war politically unpalatable, possibly untenable, in the USA.

### The Effects of the War

The total number of people killed was almost certainly well over 3 million – possibly more like 4 million – in a nation whose population was some 30 million when the war started. Although these figures may seem high, if one takes into account the almost unbelievable intensity of the bombing, the shortage of medical facilities, the lack of food and the extreme cold and lack of shelter in the context of a scorched-earth policy and the systematic destruction of livestock, they are not implausible.

By far the largest number of people died in North Korea, but neither North Korea nor China will say how many (they may not know exactly). Our estimate is that over 2 million North Korean civilians died and about 500,000 North Korean soldiers. In addition, some 1 million Chinese soldiers probably died (though one first-hand Chinese source has put the figure at 3 million). South Korean civilian deaths were about 1 million; Southern battle-related deaths were some 47,000; non-battle-related military deaths were probably higher. US deaths are put at 54,246, of whom 33,629

**Pyongyang at the end of the war.**

were 'battle deaths'. The total number of battle deaths among other forces came to 3,194, of whom 686 were British. The highest death and casualty rates among UN forces were suffered by the Turks, Greeks and French.

The reactions of the two sides reveal the strange nature of the war. Each side proclaims that it won, yet each actually seems to feel that it lost. In its own terms, each side is right. The communist position is that the USA and Rhee started the war in order to destroy North Korea (and, perhaps, attack China or Russia, or both), therefore the communists won a victory by preventing this; in addition, it was a victory of a different kind to inflict on the USA the first major defeat in its history. The US–UN position is that since North Korea (or, possibly, Stalin) started the war, the US–UN won a victory by 'deterring aggression' and preventing the overthrow of Rhee.

During the war itself, in January 1952, General Van Fleet said, 'Korea has been a blessing. There had to be a Korea either here or some place in the world.' But Mark Clark, who signed the armistice, wrote in his memoirs of his 'personal disappointment that my government did not find it expedient to whip the communists thoroughly in our first shooting war with them'. Many figures in the West claim the war could – and should – have been 'won'. Among these is Ronald Reagan, who told a press conference in April 1984 that MacArthur should have been allowed 'to lead us to a victory in Korea'.

North Koreans unanimously describe the war as a great victory but go further and call the armistice a 'surrender' by the USA. According to Kim Il Sung, 'In the Korean war, the US imperialists suffered an ignominious military defeat for the first time in the history of the United States; this meant the beginning of a downward path for US imperialism.' Communist sources also emphasize the fact that the Korean war discredited the myth of nuclear omnipotence. Mao called the war 'a great victory . . . mainly because ours was a people's war'.

**How the North remembers the war.** ▷
▽

In fact, neither side won outright. Both had defeats as well as victories, and political and military results were not always symmetrical. Above all, the war was an unmitigated disaster for the Korean people of North and South. The civil conflict had not been worked through but frozen by outside intervention. One of the fairest US commentators, Robert Simmons, has written: 'The intervention of the United States in the Korean Civil War had disastrous consequences both for America and for the Korean peninsula. A potentially swift and relatively bloodless reunification was converted into a carnage.'

**A poster. The text says, 'Never Forget the US Imperialists, Wolves.'**

One big winner in the war was Syngman Rhee. The US intervention saved him.

For the North the political effects of the war were ambiguous. It raised its prestige in the Third World and among anti-colonial movements, by whom it was perceived as having inflicted major defeats on the USA and resisted American (and British) occupation. But the war also greatly contributed to the long-term estrangement and isolation of the North from the Western world.

For China too the war's effects were ambivalent. It caused many deaths and much suffering. It drained resources from reconstruction. It prevented the People's Republic from taking Taiwan and reunifying the nation. And it kept China out of the UN for two decades. On the other hand, it strengthened China by showing the world that it had defeated the USA by pushing it back 200 miles from China's border.

The biggest winner of all was Chiang Kai-shek. The war saved him without his even having to fight or suffer the devastation that Korea experienced.

For the USSR, overall the war was a disaster. It allowed the USA to convince its allies and much of the Western world – on inadequate, and sometimes massaged, evidence – that Stalin was on the march and thus

**Scenes from a children's song-and-dance number, 'Let's Dismember the US Imperialists'.**

to accelerate Western rearmament, including the rearmament of both West Germany and Japan.

The Soviet Union, in a sense, ended up getting the worst of both worlds: in the West it was held responsible for the outbreak of war; in the communist camp there was resentment that it had not overtly come to the aid of its ally. Although the war served to tie China more closely to the USSR in the medium term, there is considerable evidence that China objected to having to take point position for the socialist camp against the world's number one military power, and the Korean war was an important factor in the Sino-Soviet split later. In addition, the war led to a marked slump in Soviet influence in North Korea in favour of an enhanced role for China.

Among the major nations, the one that gained the most was Japan. The outbreak of the war made a peace treaty possible, followed by independence, on highly favourable terms. The Korean war also greatly boosted economic recovery (which was already under way by 1950). Japan became a huge 'sanctuary' and vital rear area for the UN, and politically the war served to bind it much more securely to the West by blocking out much of the memory of the Pacific War.

The war had a gigantic impact on the entire Western world. According to Dean Acheson, it 'destroyed the Truman administration'. It also, less directly, destroyed the Labour government in Britain and the whole post-1945 Labour programme. But Acheson, interestingly, gave his agreement to the observation that Korea also 'came along and saved us'. Churchill, in his inimitable way, put his view bluntly near the end of the war: 'Korea does not really matter now. I'd never heard of the bloody place until I was seventy-four. Its importance lies in the fact that it has led to the re-arming of America.' It was the key factor behind the military build-up of NATO and the vast expansion of military budgets in all the major Western countries. The US army expanded from 1.5 million to 3.5 million during the war, and the military budget rose from about $15 billion in 1950 to some $50 billion a year. The war also led to a world economic boom without the high inflation that the Vietnam war caused.

Korea had a profound effect on US strategic thinking and led straight into Vietnam. In this a big role was played by Maxwell Taylor, who drew the lesson from Korea that what the USA needed was 'flexible response' – a strategy that, with Kennedy's backing, he helped to pioneer in Vietnam.

Within the USA itself the war had far-reaching effects, which have been underestimated. It was the first war the USA had fought that was unpopular both with the public and with the troops. Richard Nixon, in his 'Checkers' speech in 1952, made a point of telling his audience: 'There are 500,000 American boys over there in Korea – and they've never had it so bad.'

The war gave a huge boost to desegregation, but it also helped foster a climate of intolerance. McCarthy prospered. Some 25,000 civil servants and academics lost their jobs as the result of political persecution during the war. The Federal Bureau of Investigation set up an office in the UN to vet the staff for loyalty to the USA and exercised illegitimate powers to get suspects fired. The UN Secretary General, Trygve Lie, was a willing accomplice in these activities. Julius and Ethel Rosenberg, who were arrested immediately after the Korean war started, were executed in the electric chair in June 1953; the judge told them: 'I believe your conduct has already caused the communist aggression in Korea with the resultant casualties exceeding 50,000 Americans.' Many of the more sinister aspects of CIA experiments took off during the Korean war – particularly those to do with drugs and experiments with the mind.

Whereas the Vietnamese and Ho Chi Minh inspired considerable sympathy in the West, the nature and credentials of the Korean revolution were completely ignored. Koreans both in the North and South, not to mention Kim Il Sung, got no understanding, much less any sympathy. No students charged through the streets of Berkeley shouting, 'Kim, Kim, Kim Il Sung.'

The United Kingdom unveiled a memorial to its dead in the Korean war only in 1987. Perhaps the most famous Western portrayal of the Korean war is *M.A.S.H.*, in which Korea is in effect a displaced substitute for Vietnam. This solves the problem of what the USA was doing in Korea by keeping almost all Koreans well out of sight and isolating a few Americans in a tent, where they ruminate about sickness, sex and golf. In its evasion *M.A.S.H.* reveals a central truth about the Korean war: not just that it was anti-communist, but also that the USA could not take in even who its Korean allies were. There was little understanding shown for Korea as a nation, as a people or as a culture. In the penultimate episode of the TV

North Korean POWs
mustered for return, 'Big
Switch', summer 1953.

Western POW being
released during 'Big
Switch'.

version, nurse Hot Lips solicits ideas for a time capsule. B.J. suggests Dante's *Inferno*. Hawkeye comes up with a bottle of Cognac: 'We drink to forget.'

### After the Armistice: from Panmunjom to Geneva

The guns had stopped, but there was a problem: Rhee had refused to sign the armistice; he had agreed not to disturb it – but only for a period of ninety days, after which, he said, he regarded himself as free to start the war again. The USA turned the problem to its advantage, but with tragic long-term consequences. It gave Rhee a mutual defence treaty that was initialled by Secretary of State Dulles in Seoul in early August 1953. The USA acquired direct control of the South Korean Army and committed itself to maintaining troops in Korea. The North had agreed to postpone discussion of foreign troops in Korea until after an armistice was signed but found that, once the armistice had been signed, this issue had been pre-empted.

The USA also prevailed on its allies to issue a declaration (the so-called 'Greater Sanctions' statement) saying that they would again intervene in Korea if the South was attacked and that 'in all probability it would not be possible to confine hostilities within the frontiers of Korea.' This was taken to mean that the West would attack China.

Shortly after the armistice, the POWs were brought to the Panmunjom area, where they were placed under the control of an Indian custodial force (which had to be helicoptered in over ROK territory from Inchon because of Rhee's hostility to their presence in Korea).

Each side appeared to give a fulsome welcome to its returning heroes. But there were tensions underneath the surface. The US government was worried that many Americans – 70 per cent by one count – had in some way collaborated. There were two schools of thought: one was that this had happened because the communists were 'diabolical'; the other argued that the real reason was that the Americans had gone soft (Ronald Reagan supplied the commentary for a 1954 film espousing this line).

The USA had two concerns: to dissipate the bad impression made by American confessions in captivity, especially those concerning germ warfare; and to make sure there were no 'Manchurian candidates' among the returnees. The antidote to the confessions was to publish recantations. In October 1953 the USA presented to the UN recantations by ten former POWs who had confessed to germ warfare. The recantations were widely accepted in the West. Less observed was the fact that the majority of US prisoners who had confessed did not recant, at least in public. In many ways the recantations are as odd as the confessions.

The full story of what happened to these POWs after they were handed back has not been revealed. Their access to the press was controlled.

As for 'Manchurian candidates', the US government claimed that it had uncovered seventy-five. The USA brought 'political' and criminal

Ronald Reagan, *right*, in *Prisoner of War* (1953). In the film Reagan plays an agent who is infiltrated into the camp to uncover a US traitor among the prisoners (a recurrent theme of the time). In real life Reagan was at the time acting as an informer for the FBI in Hollywood. As President, Reagan said that MacArthur should have been allowed to 'win' in Korea.

Frank Sinatra, *left*, and Laurence Harvey, *right*, in *The Manchurian Candidate* (1960), the film that crystallized, safely long after the event, American fears about 'brainwashing'. Laurence Harvey, who is being programmed as a political assassin, is shooting a fellow POW.

Vice-President Richard Nixon receiving the key to the city of Seoul from Mayor Kim Tae Sin, 11 November 1953 (Syngman Rhee is in the background). In his memoirs Nixon includes an awed description of his meetings with Rhee, who talked of reviving the war. Nixon learnt his 'madman' theory from Rhee: act crazy so your foes will not know what to expect you to do.

charges against a number of ex-POWs, ranging from murder to lesser charges. One returnee was sentenced to life for murdering at least two sick fellow POWs by pushing them out of a hut to die in the cold. A preliminary investigation was also mounted against the senior US pilot captured who had confessed to germ warfare, Colonel Frank W. Schwable. After a while the US government seemed to stop worrying about a communist plot: 'brainwashing' and 'menticide' disappeared from sight. Instead Washington swung to the alternative explanation: that Americans had gone soft. In 1955 the Army introduced a 'Code of Conduct' that laid down what a prisoner could or could not do.

Twenty-one US prisoners and one Briton chose to go to China. Most later returned to the USA, where they were treated as 'turncoats', though the US government prosecuted only the first few.

We do not know if there were similar problems with returning North Korean POWs, but we do know something about what happened to the Chinese prisoners who returned to the mainland. They were given a warm welcome – and put under close surveillance. One concern was to uncover outright spies, of whom there were quite a number. (Some had been taken to Japan for special training.) According to Jean Pasqualini, who saw some of these men in prison in China, the agents were given life sentences, not executed. However, more generally the communists dis-

Kim Il Sung and
Vietnamese leader Ho Chi
Minh, Hanoi, November
1958. The manifest
contrast in personalities
does not explain the
different responses that
the two leaders and the
two revolutions evoked in
the West. Yet the two wars
had much in common,
including the same enemy.
Kim later visited Hanoi in
secret at least twice.

trusted former prisoners, partly because they had surrendered, partly because of the influences to which they had been subject in captivity. A survey of these men was published in a Chinese Army magazine in 1987. Party members and people in the Army and in senior jobs were demoted to menial posts; many were exiled to the countryside and rehabilitated only after the death of Mao, in some cases as late as 1981.

The armistice committed the signatories to holding talks to set up a political conference to decide the future of Korea. These opened on 25 October 1953 between the USA, represented by Arthur Dean (a partner in Dulles's law firm), China's future Foreign Minister Huang Hua and North Korea's Ki Sok Bok. They broke down on 12 December. The communists asked for an assurance that Rhee would be bound by the commitments of the political conference. They were particularly concerned about the 22,000 POWs, two-thirds of them Chinese, who had not been returned. Huang said that the USA was guilty of 'perfidy' because it refused to acknowledge that it had connived at Rhee's removal of the 27,000 POWs in June 1953. Dean stormed out of the talks and never returned. The British envoy in Peking, Humphrey Trevelyan, wrote: 'The Chinese were left in possession of the field, and, in our judgement, had won on points.' But perhaps the Americans won a more important victory by preventing a political conference from being held.

### The Geneva Conference on Korea, April–June 1954

Geneva was a unique occasion. It was the only time in post-1945 history when the foreign ministers of the five leading world states met. The conference was exceptionally long. Including the part on Indochina, it lasted three months. The Korea conference ran from 26 April to 15 June, the Indochina one from 8 May to 21 July. To some extent events in Indochina overshadowed the Korea conference, with the key French stronghold in Indochina, Dien Bien Phu, falling on 7 May.

Most Western books write off the Korea conference as of little interest and as doomed to failure. But this is not the view of most of the Western participants – nor is it what emerges from recently declassified documents. Before the conference opened a British Foreign Office document recorded: 'We understand from the US Embassy that Mr Dulles summoned the representatives of the [allies] to invite them to the conference and give them the party line.' Dulles distinguished himself right at the beginning of the conference by refusing Zhou's outstretched hand. He then departed, leaving Bedell Smith to deputize for him.

The main issues were elections and the withdrawal of foreign troops. The USA and South Korea proposed that elections be held only in North Korea, under Southern law and under UN auspices. The North proposed nationwide elections, arranged by an all-Korea electoral commission and supervised by a Neutral Nations Supervisory Commission. On the question of foreign troops, the North proposed a simultaneous and proportionate pull-out of all foreign forces before elections. The South and the USA refused this.

Eden's private secretary, Shuckburgh, wrote on 29 April, 'No reasonable proposition has yet been put forward from the Western side.' On 4 May he wrote in his diary: 'The conference is stalled . . . and . . . it is the fault of the non-communists. (On Korea, the Americans have not yet induced Syngman Rhee to agree to any plan remotely acceptable to the rest of us).' The Canadian Ronning wrote later: 'I was appalled by the great differences in position being taken by the United States and South Korea on the one hand and by most of the rest of us on the other.' The USA, isolated with South Korea, fell back on the argument that the North had to accept UN supervision of elections. Because the UN was a belligerent, this was unacceptable to the North. Ronning wrote later words that summed up the real (though unspoken) feelings of many Western delegates: 'The United States delegation was instructed by the State Department to break up the conference on the issue of United Nations authority . . . [which] to me was rank hypocrisy . . . The [UN] issue was trumped up to break up the conference; the authority of the United Nations was phoney.' This is true, as Geneva had been specifically set up as a non-UN conference.

When Belgium's Paul-Henri Spaak tried to reach a compromise with Zhou towards the end Bedell Smith raised his arm and cut him off. The French delegate Chauvel wrote of that occasion: 'The Americans torpedoed the debate shamelessly.' Ronning's conclusions are:

The communists had come to Geneva to negotiate . . . I thought I had come to participate in a peace conference . . . Instead, the emphasis was entirely on preventing a peace settlement from being realized . . . There was no excuse for closing the conference without a peace agreement. Molotov's resolution . . . could have been accepted as a basis for a settlement by most of the Sixteen [states that fought under the UN flag].

Much has been written about the start of the war but much less on how it ended and why Korea was not reunified. There is room for honest disagreement on how it started, but there can be no question that Rhee was against ending it. The USA maintained Rhee in power at the cost of keeping Korea divided.

The conference was a turning-point in Atlantic relations. When the USA tried to reconstitute the Korea coalition for Indochina, it failed. The only countries the USA could get to fight in Vietnam for the Emperor Bao Dai ('the poor man's Syngman Rhee', as one Geneva newspaper called him) were the Asian Pacific Rim states – of which much the most important, in terms of military assistance, was South Korea. Ultimately what emerged from Geneva was the South-East Asia Treaty Organization (SEATO), a pale echo of NATO and a poor substitute for the broad anti-communist coalition that Dulles had tried to assemble.

Geneva was the only international conference of its kind that North Korea has ever attended; but it failed to crack the Western bloc in the way that China did, or the Vietnamese did later.

### Divided Korea since the War

Since the end of the war both North and South Korea have evolved distinctive states within a nation that has maintained a very strong sense of its identity and in which the two societies are less different than the two regimes that have governed them. Both have enjoyed vigorous growth by Third World standards; both have also very large military and security forces. While the South has remained closely tied to the Western world, economically and militarily, the North has become a member of the Non-aligned Movement, while remaining within the communist world.

In the South Syngman Rhee remained President until he was overthrown by popular demonstrations in April 1960 as he tried to rig yet another election. There followed a short period of relative freedom for about one year. During this interval many of the trends that came to the surface again in 1987 were visible: students called for a return to Panmunjom in order to re-open direct talks with the North; workers demonstrated for trades-union rights; and there were calls to open the files on the Korean war.

In May 1961 the Army stepped in and staged a *coup*, under General Park Chung-hee. Park was a former officer in the Japanese Imperial

Syngman Rhee with South Vietnamese leader Ngo Dinh Diem, 18 September 1957. Rhee tried to link South Korea and South Vietnam closely as early as 1953. Later the South Korean Army supported the USA in Indochina, sending a total of 312,000 men, including future presidents Chon Doo-hwan (1980–88) and Roh Tae-woo (1988– ).

Army who had spent his early career chasing fellow-Koreans, anti-Japanese guerrillas, in Manchuria. He presided over a period of spectacular economic growth, aided by tight political controls, until he was shot to death over dinner in 1979 by the head of his own CIA.

Pyongyang, 1958: a woman looks at a poster of Russia's sputnik.

Another very brief period of relative freedom ensued. The military soon intervened again to stage a *coup* under Chon Doo-hwan, an intelligence general who commanded a paratroop regiment in Vietnam, fighting alongside the USA.

The South, with a population of about 42 million, has been transformed since the end of the Korean war. Gross National Product and per capita income rose by about twenty times between 1953 and 1986 (per capita income from about US$50 to about US$2,000). The South has broken into many key sectors of highly advanced industry, producing high-quality goods and with a broadly based industrial structure. Both the economic geography and the social composition of the country have changed enormously.

South Korea has one of the largest military forces on the globe, with approximately 600,000 people under arms. The whole continent

of South America, which is hardly short of overblown armies, has about 800,000 people in the armed forces, with about eight times the population. Up to 1987 economic gains had not been matched by political progress. The society remains very male-dominated and, in spite of a large Christian population, in many ways very Confucian.

There is a strong US military presence. After 1953 the USA gradually withdrew most of its armed forces but kept the Southern Army under its command (it is the only foreign armed force in the world under direct US control). In 1957 the USA announced that it would no longer recognize the authority of the Neutral Nations Supervisory Commission,

**Rebuilding Pyongyang in 1958: taken by French photographer and film-maker Chris Marker, one of the shots in a book of his remarkable photographs entitled *Coréennes*, a unique record of North Korea at the time.**

which had been set up to supervise compliance with the armistice, and that it regarded itself as at liberty to bring in new armaments, including nuclear weapons. There are currently approximately 41,000 US military personnel in South Korea, with nuclear weapons. South Korea is the only place in the world where nuclear weapons are used to deter a non-nuclear force.

The North has set up a tight, security-conscious regime that considers itself a leader of the Third World, blessed with the good luck to be led by a political genius, Kim Il Sung, who is the longest-lasting non-hereditary leader in the world, having been in power effectively since 1945. The regime's picture of itself as a 'paradise on earth' is at sharp variance with the view widely held in the West, which is that it is a bleak, backward workhouse run by a megalomaniac tyrant.

The truth is more complex. The North is a more successful socialist economy than is generally recognized; per capita income has risen from a negligible figure in 1953 to a level that is probably about US$1,500. The regime has been fairly successful in delivering social and economic gains to its population, even with very large military budgets and armed forces. It is a dictatorship in a mould that is Confucian as well as communist. It is also in many ways authentically nationalist and 'national'. Among foreigners Kim Il Sung's obnoxious cult of the personality brings derision and discredit on him and his government. Given the degree of censorship and control within the society, it is impossible to know what people really think about him and the regime, but it is probable that he commands respect. To some extent this may be the result of isolating the population from information and the massive fabrication of history, but it may also derive from the fact that he fought against the Japanese in extremely tough conditions and has given the population of the North a form of political and social stability known to few nations on earth. Kim Il Sung, who was born in 1912, has attempted to ensure continuity by endorsing his eldest son, Kim Jong Il, who was officially born in 1942, as his successor.

The North has tried to make itself as self-reliant as possible (which is not the same as self-sufficient) in every field. It collectivized agriculture immediately after the Korean war. Compared with that in other communist countries, this process was relatively uncontentious, as so many of the boundaries demarcating property (as well as the owners) had been obliterated by American bombing.

There are no foreign troops or nuclear weapons in the North. The last Chinese forces withdrew in 1958 after putting in a major reconstruction effort, which was one of the keys to the North's very fast recovery after the war. The North has large armed forces – how large is the subject of dispute, but the figure is probably about 600,000.

The North has made a big point of its independence. Kim has maintained a balance between, and some distance from, his two giant neighbours, the USSR and China. In 1975 Pyongyang became a member of the Non-aligned Movement and now considers itself as much a member of the Third World bloc as of the communist camp.

The USA maintains its toughest economic embargo *vis-à-vis* any state in the world on North Korea. Most major Western states have no diplomatic relations with Pyongyang. This long-term attempt at isolation reflects powerful and unresolved psychological and political issues left over from the Korean war.

There have been many incidents along the Demilitarized Zone since 1953. Well over 1,000 people were killed between the armistice and the end of 1985. The biggest US–North Korean imbroglio came in 1968, when the North seized a US spy ship, the *Pueblo*, off the coast, killing one American sailor and setting off a furore in the USA.

In 1969, within a few months of Nixon's taking office as President, the North Koreans shot down a US plane, killing all thirty-one people on board. Nixon and Kissinger at first recommended dropping a nuclear bomb on the North but later backed off.

### What Chance Reunification?

Reunification is still at the centre of Korean national life. Over forty years of division have not changed this. The division is felt as bitterly and as sadly as ever. Almost every family in Korea has a missing relative on the other side, and these broken family ties are keenly felt. With one exception, a brief exchange of visits by one small group from each side in 1985, there has been no contact between the inhabitants of North and South, no

Pyongyang skyline, 1985. ▷

Kim Il Sung's son and heir-designate, Kim Jong Il, *right*, and Defence Minister O Jin U, *second right*, examining new uniforms for women members of the People's Army. Kim Jong Il stands second in the Party hierarchy and O Jin U third. Women make up about 10 per cent of the People's Army. During the Korean War they fought in the front lines.

**Religion in the service of both sides.**

*Above left*: **A Maltese bishop at a North Korean book show. The North Koreans churn out unbelievable quantities of Kim Il Sung's works and glossy (and tacky) propaganda magazines. They obsessively photograph people looking at their publications and frequently reproduce them as 100 per cent devotees of the cult of Kim, often without their knowledge and approval.**

*Above right*: **Christ in the Sky. This picture was published in an American newspaper that said it had been taken by a US pilot during an air battle and that when it was developed the face of Christ appeared.**

postal service, no telephone. It has been a criminal offence in the South to try to make contact with anyone in the North (it may also be an offence in the North).

On 4 July 1972 North and South published a joint communiqué calling for national reconciliation, steps towards reunification and the removal of 'foreign interference'. The attempt collapsed when South Korea refused to discuss the withdrawal of US troops, claiming that these were not 'foreign' because technically they came under UN command. North–South talks continued spasmodically through the 1980s.

There are two big problems. One is that North and South have no agreement between themselves terminating the civil war. The North signed the armistice in 1953 – with the USA. The North has proposed to the USA that the armistice be converted into a peace treaty. The USA says that it will not negotiate without the South. The North wants US troops to leave. The USA and the South do not. The North says that it is willing to negotiate a peace pact with the South separately if US troops undertake to leave and it has proposed neutralization of the peninsula. The South and the USA say that they do not trust the North.

Each year US and South Korean forces carry out joint military manoeuvres known as 'Operation Team Spirit', which last over two months. They have grown from fewer than 50,000 troops to well over 200,000 and are the second largest military manoeuvres anywhere in the world, involving planning for nuclear war and amphibious landings. The North says that they are an obstacle to negotiations.

Another key consideration is how to find a way to dissolve the decades of tension and distrust between North and South. The South, with twice the population of the North, is naturally keen to turn this demographic superiority to its advantage in any reunification process. The

North's proposals stress 'great national unity' and have tended to seek ways to circumvent the regime in the South, which, it claims, has not been representative of the population (the Southern regime says the same about the Northern regime). The two regimes are far apart on ways to achieve both reconciliation and reunification.

Leaving aside any moral judgement on the two regimes, there are important differences that affect their approach to reunification. In the North Kim Il Sung presides over a strong, centralized government whose control over the population is firm. The situation in the South is different. When Park was seriously challenged by Kim Dae-jung, the Korean CIA kidnapped Kim in Tokyo and beat him up; he was then sentenced to death (the sentence was not carried out) on trumped-up charges. The troops Chon used in his *Putsch* had fought under him in Vietnam, where they acquired a reputation for brutality. In spring 1980 the same paratroop unit put down a popular uprising in the city of Kwangju with great cruelty. Torture has been widely used – and this was a major factor in detonating the popular demonstrations in 1987.

The North and the South each claims for itself the right to represent the whole of Korea. Neither has a seat in the United Nations. The West has suggested 'cross-recognition' – that is, that China and the USSR recognize South Korea in return for the USA's and Japan's recognition of North Korea, and that both North Korea and South Korea be admitted to the UN. The North has rejected this on the grounds that it would help to perpetuate the division of the nation. US proposals tend to focus on international diplomatic arrangements; North Korean proposals tend to appeal to national reconciliation and to concentrate on an intra-Korean solution.

Is reunification possible? We believe it is. Korea has exceptional ethnic, cultural and linguistic unity. In 1945, at the time of the Japanese surrender, there was far less vengeance on collaborators (with far greater excuse) than there was in France in 1944. Again in 1987 there was extraordinarily little revenge against police agents and those involved in torture.

Nor is the relationship between the North and the South as closed as many foreigners think. In 1948 most of the political leaders in the South went to meet the Northern leaders in Pyongyang to try to stave off separate elections in the South and to preserve the nation's unity: such a move would have been unthinkable in Germany in 1948. In 1960–61, during the brief period of liberalization in the South, students and workers called for meetings at Panmunjom and met an enthusiastic response. The events of 1987 showed that the desire for reunification is as strong as ever, and reunification is a key plank in the platform of most parties.

A united Korea would be a nation of over 60 million people, bigger than that of France or Britain. Given the achievements of both North and South and the obvious complementarity of their economies, as well as the psychological impetus that reunification would bring, all indications are that a united Korea would have a lot going for it.

**Peace at last: dancing, North Korea, 1958.**

218

Korea has been the victim of a tragic historical injustice. At the end of World War II it was the only state not responsible for aggression which became divided. Japan, which had occupied and annexed Korea and attacked its neighbours, was not split. Even Austria had its unity restored as the Cold War faded in Europe. Most cruel of all is rhetoric to the effect that Korea is 'a dagger pointed at Japan': this is the exact opposite of the truth. Korea has never attacked any other country. Rather, it has repeatedly been the victim of attack and interference. It has a right to be left alone, in peace, as a single nation.

# PHOTOGRAPHIC ACKNOWLEDGEMENTS

For permission to reproduce the photographs in this book grateful acknowledgement is made to the following: the *Age*, Melbourne, p. 94 (photograph by Alan
Lambert, published 1950); Major W. Ellery Anderson, MBE, MC and bar, p. 150
(centre right); AP/World Wide Photos, p. 110 (bottom); Associated Press, pp.
120, 178–9; BBC Hulton Picture Library, frontispiece and pp. 70, 76, 92, 97, 98–9,
100 (top and bottom), 102; Margaret Briggs, c/o Associated Press, p. 67
(published in *National Geographic*, February 1950); Camera Press, 104; Colorific!,
pp. 41, 42 (photographs by Carl Mydans, *Life Magazine*, copyright © Time, Inc.,
1948), 146–7, 148–9, 149 (photographs by Margaret Bourke-White, *Life Magazine*,
copyright © Time, Inc., 1952; Bruce Cumings, p. 53 (left); Kate Fleron, pp. 136,
138 (top), 139, 141; William Gaines, pp. 89, 123, 174 (copyright © William
Gaines, 1988); Professor Franco Graziosi, pp. 184–5; A. B. Jamieson, p. 63;
Keystone, Paris, p. 217 (right); Vitali S. Latov, pp. 151 (top), 168, 170, 184 (top),
189; Major General Nikolai Georgievich Lebedev, p. 28 (bottom); Chris Marker,
pp. 213, 214–15, 218–19; Tibor Meray, pp. 167, 185 (top); the late Colonel F. S. B.
Peach, p. 64; Popperfoto, pp. 14, 53 (right), 65, 101 (bottom), 103, 116 (top), 128,
131 (top), 134–5 (right), 173; Lucjan Pracki/Wojskowa Agencija Fotograficzna
Archiwum, Warsaw, pp. 169 (top and bottom), 176, 186; Nina Prescod, pp. 72,
84, 88, 89, 123, 157 (top left), 174, 183; Public Record Office, London, p. 195;
Réunion des Musées Nationaux, Paris, p. 140 (copyright © DACF, 1987); Solo
Syndication and Literary Agency Ltd Daily Mail, p. 69; Swen Publications, New
York, p. 83; Walter Sullivan, p. 49 (top and bottom); Metro-Goldwyn-Mayer,
p. 207 (top, from *Prisoner of War*, copyright © 1954 by Loew's Inc., ren. 1982 by
Metro-Goldwyn-Mayer Film Co.); M.C. Productions, p. 207 (bottom, from *The
Manchurian Candidate*, copyright © M.C. Productions, 1962); United Nations, p.
190; US Air Force, pp. 129 (top), 145 (top and bottom), 188, 196; US Archives, pp.
19 (left and right), 20, 22 (top and bottom), 23, 25, 26, 31 (top and bottom), 32, 33
(top), 35, 37, 38–9, 45, 46 (top and bottom), 47, 55 (top), 61, 79 (all pictures), 85, 86,
87, 93, 101 (top), 107, 108 (all pictures), 111, 113, 114, 115, 116 (bottom), 126–7,
128–9 (bottom), 131 (bottom), 133, 134 (left), 137, 138 (bottom), 142, 150 (top), 152,
153, 154–5 (top and bottom), 161, 162, 163, 164–5, 171 (bottom), 175, 177, 182, 187,
192 (bottom), 205 (top and bottom), 208; US Army, pp. 75, 92, 105 (right), 109,
150 (bottom), 158; US Army Signal Corps, pp. 39 (top), 40 (top), 106 (top and
bottom), 110 (top), 132–3, 137; George Weidenfeld and Nicolson/Arthur Barker
Ltd, p. 68; Max Whitby, p. 171 (top); Xinhua (New China News Agency), pp. 122
(top and bottom), 125 (top and bottom), 130, 166, 199 (top).

# INDEX

Caption entries are indicated in **bold** type.

# ABOUT THE AUTHORS

Jon Halliday is the originator and writer of the PBS television series on which this book is based. In preparing the project he traveled to many countries, including North Korea, China, and the USSR. He has written extensively on Korea and is the author and editor of seven books, which have been translated into twelve languages.

Bruce Cumings is a professor of East Asian history at the University of Chicago. He is the author of the two-volume work *The Origins of the Korean War*. He has contributed articles on East Asia to the *New York Times*, the *Nation*, the *New York Review of Books*, and many other publications.